JAILBREAK

A Slow Journey Round Eastern Europe

Gill Suttle

SCIMITAR PRESS

SCIMITAR PRESS
P.O. Box 41, Monmouth, Gwent, NP5 3UH.

© Gill Suttle 1998

British Library Cataloguing in Publication Data
A catalogue record for this book is
available from the British Library

ISBN 0 9534536 0 X

Typeset, printed & bound in Great Britain by
Zenith Media,
Zenith House, Moy Road Industrial Estate,
Taffs Well, Cardiff.

In memory of

my mother, Judy Suttle

*a tower of strength whose love and support preserved
my sanity through the early years of illness*

CONTENTS

ACKNOWLEDGEMENTS

Special thanks to Rob Dean for his immensely detailed proof-reading and comments - not to mention giving me the benefit of his extensive computing know-how. Also to Philippa Roberts and Benedict Kolczynski, who proof-read the final version.

A big thankyou, too, to Jenny Stratton for her invaluable help in designing the cover.

Thankyou to those authors and publishers who have permitted quotations:

John Murray (Publishers) Ltd: "Between the Woods and the Water", by Patrick Leigh Fermor.
Dr. Clare Fleming: "The Glass Cage". This article was first published in the British Medical Journal in 1994, no. 308, p. 797.
Clare Francis and Dr. Anne Macintyre: foreword to "ME and How to Live With It", by Dr. Anne Macintyre.
Canongate: "Mountaineering in Scotland", by W.H. Murray.
Harper Collins: "The Hobbit", by J.R.R. Tolkien.
Curtis Brown: "The Wind in the Willows", by Kenneth Grahame, copyright The University Chest, Oxford, reproduced by permission of Curtis Brown, London.
G. N. C.: "The Prophet", by Kahlil Gibran. Copyright holder: Gibran National Committee P.O.Box 116/5487 Beirut, Lebanon. Fax (9611) 396916, e mail: k.gibran@cyberia.netib
A.M. Heath: "Animal Farm", by George Orwell.
Peter Avery: Translation of "The Ruba'iyat of Omar Khayyam", published by Penguin Books.

INTRODUCTION

The tyre was Definitely Deceased. I stood in the rain and stared at it gloomily, considering the options.

I could have changed it in ten minutes flat... five years ago. Nowadays, things were different, which was why I had taken out the most extensive Breakdown and Recovery service I could find.

The problem was, it was no use without a phone. And half a mile outside a tiny, sleepy village on the Polish-Belorussian border, I had about as much chance of finding one as of lighting a fire under the downpour to make smoke signals.

It was Saturday evening. The post office would be closed; and the chance of finding a phone at a private house in this rather backward area was remote. And then there was the walk back to the village. I could have run it in minutes... five years ago. But this was now, and it would cost me half an hour and a soaking. Moreover, if I returned to the van unsuccessful, it would be next day before I could resume normal service and address the wheel.

Attempting to change it myself looked marginally less horrible. After all, someone was bound to stop and help if I looked hopelessly incompetent - not unusual, nowadays.

I began to hunt reluctantly for the wheelbrace. What the HELL, I wondered, was I doing in this God-forsaken place anyway?

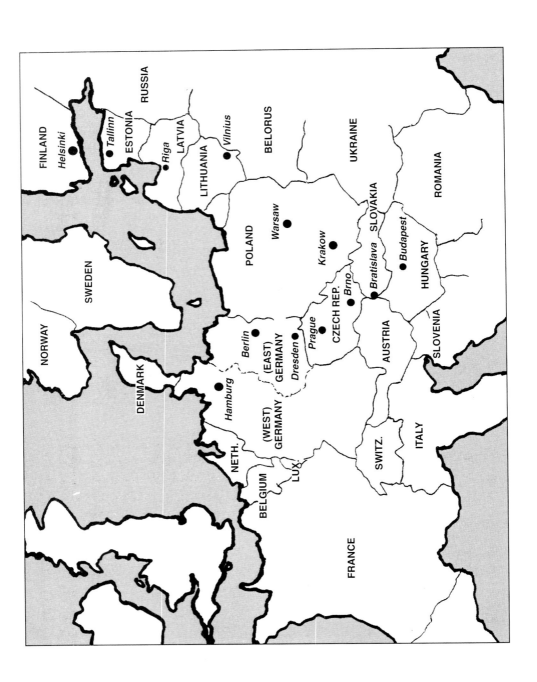

CHAPTER I: LET'S TWIST AGAIN

The road goes ever on and on,

Down from the door where it began.

Now far ahead the road has gone,

And I must follow if I can...

(J.R.R. Tolkien)

"Of course," I'd written to a friend, "if I have a relapse in Ruritania, a seizure in Silesia - or even a puncture in Poland - I might never be heard of again!"

A few years ago, when ME meant nothing more sinister than Middle East, and my idea of travel was a packed rucksack and a plane ticket to Damascus or Cairo, driving around Europe would have seemed a bit tame. That was before illness descended, and my world imploded. Travel vanished instantly from the agenda, soon to be followed by work. My horizons closed in to just beyond bed and sofa.

Now, however, after years of frustration and isolation, they were beginning to recede again. How far was by no means clear, but it was definitely to somewhere beyond my current field of view. High time to get off my posterior and find out, before I ended up stir crazy.

Clearly, any attempt to break out would need careful planning. Although I could now stay out of bed for four hours at a time, I still couldn't walk more than a few hundred yards, and carrying luggage was out of the question. I could forget any ideas of trekking in the Himalayas, or riding a bike to Samarkand. Instead, it was necessary to plan from the other end, by setting out what I could do, and finding something to fit the limitations.

On the plus side, I could still drive; in fact, almost the whole of my active life for the last few years had revolved, so to speak, about my wheels. And with this thought, inspiration struck.

A motor caravan!

If I was still pretty much imprisoned by my bed, the path to increased mobility was to make the jailer itself mobile. With means to transport self, all material needs and bed, I could be completely self-sufficient. The cage could

3

be forced well and truly open.

And anyway, my dear old Ford, now starting round the clock for the second time, had been living on borrowed time for years. I would soon be forced to change my vehicle, and what better than to replace it with something perfectly fitted to the requirements of a new lifestyle?

A look at the classified sections of the motoring weeklies, however, sent my hopes collapsing like a damp soufflé. Even the smallest of these golden coaches either cost over five figures, or was so old that even the upholstery was in danger of rusting. The message was painfully clear: you don't buy such mobile luxury on Invalidity Benefit and a small teaching pension.

There had to be an affordable alternative.

Some homework on minivans provided the answer. The little 970cc Bedford Rascal, at around a couple of thousand pounds second-hand and doing 35-50mpg, was pocket-sized to buy and run, as well as just to look at. Moreover, with an interior measuring six feet by four, it would be just big enough to take a mattress.

Its neat, clean lines sat alluringly on the pages of the glossy brochure. It was love at first sight. I couldn't wait to form an alliance with this beguiling match-box toy. Together, we would travel far and wide; the world would become our oyster.

With the New Year, I began to scheme.

*

There was no question as to where to go.

In 1989 my attention, with that of the world, had been fixed on events in eastern Europe. I had watched in fascination as the Communist megalith had crashed to the ground and shattered, and the world I had known all my life was redesigned. Various friends had jumped on the plane to Berlin, to trample on the rubble of its Wall and share in an ecstasy of rejoicing; while I had looked on from within my strait-jacket and ground my teeth in a jealous fury.

Now was the chance to put things straight. I would go and see for myself; and make up for the wasted time by travelling as widely as possible through the former Soviet satellites.

The more I thought about it, the better the idea seemed. Whereas western motorways are often congested, with the additional hazard of drivers such as the French and Italians, car ownership in the east was still limited, and traffic would be light. Moreover, newly fledged market economies were bound to ensure a favourable exchange rate, making for cheaper living. With economy the watchword in all things, not least effort, eastwards was the perfect direction.

I began to spend evenings in front of the fire, poring over the atlas. The former Communist countries began, it transpired, nearer to home than I had thought, for Berlin was only a couple of hours' drive from the Hamburg ferry. Within days a rough route was taking shape almost of its own volition, as a live thing. Berlin could only be followed by the beautiful cities of Dresden and Prague, whence I must of course continue into Hungary, a land which, for the fame of its horses and horsemen, I had long wished to visit. From here the best direction was north across Slovakia into Poland, so as to keep within reach of the Baltic ferries for the homeward journey. Finally, having come so far, it would be inexcusable not to go on and see the Baltic states; especially when I discovered that a ferry from Helsinki travelled the length of the Baltic and docked within a few miles of Hamburg.

That was the easy bit. If only the rest of the planning were as simple. But there was one very good reason, at least, why it wouldn't be.

*

For a description of ME and its effects, please turn to the Appendix

*

To live with ME is to live in a looking-glass world, in which normal rules are regularly inverted. It is a world in which to go for a walk in the fresh air, rather than clearing the mind, may blur the vision within a few steps; where regular exercise can steadily undermine, rather than steadily strengthening. The work ethic of a lifetime must be unlearned, because it is not virtuous but self-destructive to get up early, or knock off half an hour's work in twenty minutes. It is acquiescence and idleness that now get the Brownie Points. And Brownie Points, failing a better sort of yardstick, are an essential part of the coping strategy, of balancing rest and exercise.

Imagine living on a very low income, permanently in the red, and surviving by credit-card. Then, for financial, read physical resources. You are living in overdraft; and, the deeper the debt, the higher the interest rate - sorry, crash-coefficient - and the longer it takes to pay what you owe.

Worse, as with plastic money, it is possible - often, indeed, necessary - to overspend on reserves you don't have, until the awful moment comes when the bill drops through the letterbox with a dull thud and you find out just how prodigal you've really been.

For in ME some, at least, of the body feed-back can be disastrously delayed. One of the banana skins it throws down is the fact that an exertion (be it visiting the supermarket or merely writing a postcard) which may cause only a manageable degree of fatigue at the time, might not exact its full revenge for a day, week or even a month. So it is never enough to listen to your body, and stop only when you feel you can't go on. That is far too late; for you must expect the after-effects of the least effort to continue to intensify, like those of sunburn, long after the exposure is ended. "You're like a microwave," says my friend Josie. "You keep cooking well after you're switched off!"

This time-lag is the worst barrier to understanding and managing the illness in the early years. Time and again you're seduced into over-confidence resulting in crash-landing; where the excesses of last month may call you to account at the same time as those of last week, yesterday and five minutes ago, in a sort of simultaneous pile-up like a sonic bang.

So you ride a switchback, in a relentless cycle of boom and bust until the lesson finally clicks. You stop saying, "Last week I was doing so well; what went wrong?" Instead you sit down and work out your average output; then spend your days endlessly totting up, earnestly counting out black marks, like a school monitor, for each exertion. Life becomes one long game of Pontoon. The awful threat of going "bust" is implicit in the rules, so you add up your cards with desperate precision, and "twist" or "stick" accordingly.

"Twist" or "stick"? Stick is safe; but if you stick you lose out, you eventually mummify. If you twist you may bust. You never quite know what the next card is. Worse, you can only guess what it *would* have been. So you learn only the hard way, by your crunching mistakes, and not by what you get right.

So you still succumb to the temptation of that evening out, or the dire urgency of mucking out the bathroom. But at least you to begin to have an idea what that will cost, and may plan accordingly. The randomness is always there, but you can flatten the switchback a little.

Better, you learn to manipulate; to nurse the boom, like an athlete peaking for your own personal Olympics, to encompass something really worthwhile... and then damn the consequences. As an ongoing strategy, that would be suicidal, as each consequent bust could mean serious relapse, and months if not years out of your useful life. But as a once-off, for a really special occasion, it could be worth the risk.

Twist or stick? There was only one way I could find out. Go for it.

*

I was one of the luckier ones, the second generation of ME sufferers. Nobody tried to psycho-analyse me, nobody even told me to pull myself together. Directly, that is; though one or two former friends took a visible step back, and a GP told me I was perfectly fit to go running over the Malvern Hills.

For "luck" in this context is relative. My tests, of course, were blank (even today, there is no test for ME, which is therefore diagnosed by eliminating other possible causes of illness), and "cardiac neurosis" appeared on my medical records. Needled by the open contempt of the consultant, I set out to prove my credentials in the only way I knew: to fight the illness, tooth and claw.

Nobody warned me - and, indeed, few doctors then knew - of the urgency of rest in the early stages, the greatly increased tendency to chronicity among those who stagger on, lowering their heads to charge The Beast mindlessly, in full frontal assault, rather than overcoming it with subtlety and patience.

Recently extremely fit from competitive sport and hillwalking, I was partly cushioned at first from the full impact of ME on my strength and stamina. It was too easy, too tempting, to believe that I could force my way through it somehow; that this thing wasn't going to beat me. Besides, I had a lot to lose by capitulation: a newly arranged teaching exchange to Australia, still a full year away, might go down the drain if I took a term off. A lot could happen in a year.

A lot did. After six months I was reduced to part-time work and after six more threw in the towel, defeated as much by the stairs at school as by fear of impending professional incompetence. By then the damage was done, and I continued to slide for another year, until bottoming out marginally and mercifully on the right side of total incapacity.

Quickly exhausting the suggestions of conventional medicine, I turned, like most, to the world of holistic therapy, though with limited success. It was learning to manage the illness properly that was my open sesame; to hoard my sparse resources and shop around for the best value from my skin-tight energy budget. After three decades of treating my body like some souped-up sports car that I could throw around all over the place at high speed, I must now see it as a rusty old barrow with its one wheel about to drop off. In the complex world of human emotions, this was no easy lesson.

Tolerance of idleness, it appeared, is an inborn talent rather than an acquired art. It's no good chaining yourself to the bed for the necessary rest period, only to lie there chewing the blankets and sweating with frustration. Far better to give in and go for a walk. But, paradoxically, it was in an inflexible regime that I finally achieved a degree of resignation, and freedom from constant inner conflict. As every parent knows, the best way to avoid arguments about bedtime is to be consistent.

Through trial and error, the rules wrote themselves. It felt a bit like being in borstal. Four hours out of bed morning and evening. Four hours "porridge", or sentence of bed, every afternoon. No remission for good behaviour, unless it be an enhancing of quality of those few hours' parole. Two walks a week, not more than half a mile, or their equivalent - a supermarket trip, say. No lifting, no hurrying, no undue exertion. And no cheating; whereas a weight-watcher may scoff the occasional doughnut without breaking the scales, or a bored athlete can take the odd day off training, a moment's self-indulgence could cost me a week in the cooler.

With the years, it got easier... as the old memories of health and fitness faded and the new regime became ingrained; as my old sports clubs stopped sending fixture lists and subscription demands; as my two horses grew older and stiffer, and more resigned to their enforced retirement; and as my dearly loved mountains of Scotland floated away on an invisible tectonic plate to the far side of my world.

*

Now, some years on, the rule-book was losing the odd page. But there was no room for complacency. To extract optimum value from any gallivanting abroad, I would have to squeeze tighter than ever the usual parsimony of my daily life, and hoard each drop of strength as jealously as miser's gold.

So, among the essential preparations for travelling, the first requirement was to pre-empt any waste of energy on needs which could be met in advance. I wanted all my legpower for exploration and enjoyment, not for going in search of material wants.

First things first. One of my early lessons in managing ME was that to reach my destination in need of a loo, only to find that the nearest was two hundred yards in the wrong direction, was inept - particularly so when my maximum range on foot was four hundred yards!

Someone offered a Portaloo. I hesitated; ideal, perhaps, but the thought of driving around with a part-full chemical toilet didn't grab me. Then... "What would happen if you had to brake suddenly?" said Josie. That did it. I would settle for an emergency bucket which could be emptied at once, furtively over a municipal flower bed if a drain wasn't near to hand.

Water - for intake, that is - presented no problems. I acquired a five gallon drum which would last several days, used sparingly. No matter that this was ten times what I could actually lift. Filled in situ by means of fifteen feet of hose with a squashy tap fitting, and placed on the floor with its tap towards the door, it would fill my four-pint containers without even being tipped.

The biggest labour was food. Of course, I intended wherever possible to try the local talent, but only if it lay in my path. I couldn't afford to go hunting. Shopping is a pain at the best of times; but there must be rations to last, if necessary, the duration. For three months, I filled an extra bag on every shopping trip: four tins, that is, or their equivalent in weight.

The menu was simple: mostly baked beans, tuna, tinned corn and a variety of tinned stews. As far as possible, for lightness and ease of acquisition, I took dried food: muesli, cereals and a monster pack of porridge oats. Also teabags, of course, and a jar of instant hot chocolate, a luxury which was all too soon exhausted. And twenty-four pints of long-life milk, which I subsequently stowed all around the inaccessible cavities too small to be good for packing otherwise.

Personal packing was facilitated by my comprehensive Travel List, compiled over many years and covering all possible needs from ice-axe to knitting needles, midge cream to anti-malarials. Only one or two items needed to be added. For personal security, a siren alarm. For that of the van, a crooklock and an ingenious device called a "Wasp", which hung on the steering wheel and responded with ear-splitting decibels to any attempt at a break-in. It was to cause me frequent embarrassment in the early days, when I often forgot to disarm it immediately, and battered the eardrums of many a good burgher of eastern Europe (not to mention my own).

The best, and easiest part of getting ready was the bit which I did on my back... reading. The Lonely Planet and Rough Guides gripped me like the latest thriller.

A precise itinerary was unadventurous, but essential. Return ferries must be pre-booked, and I wasn't capable of forced marches to make up lost time. More, without rigid plans, I would certainly be lured off course by every tempting topographical titbit along the way, attempt far too much, and collapse like a pricked balloon at the end of a week. If I was intending to heave my unco-operative carcass over four thousand miles, it must be seriously humoured, and the demands on it planned to the last calorie. So for good measure, I wrote into the schedule a "rest day", which would stay completely empty, once a week.

Gradually, the pile of books took over the bedroom floor. And it was always the same one at the bottom.

Since there wasn't much hope of swotting up the rudiments of half-a-dozen languages in three months, I opted to knock some of the rust off my German, a universal second language in eastern Europe. From a friend in my Russian class (that might be useful in the Baltic states, I thought, when the germ of the idea had first sprouted) I borrowed a thriller in German. Hard going, but the most painless way to broaden vocabulary. I slogged through it doggedly with the help of a dictionary, which was in tatters by the end. But in the weeks to come, that bit of homework was to prove invaluable.

There was a lot of necessary deskwork. First and foremost, I wrote to the embassies of the countries on the route, to check on motoring rules and regulations, essential papers and visas. The last was simple; under the rapidly changing circumstances, most former Communist countries were busily revoking visa requirements for U.K. citizens. Only Latvia remained bureaucratically obdurate; but before my departure it, too, had followed the herd. For driving, I must have an international licence, green card and a few extra odds and ends such as a fire extinguisher.

Comprehensive Breakdown and Recovery insurance was a *sine qua non*. Since the onset of illness I had been unable to undertake even such a simple task as changing a wheel. I could forget about executing a solo push start, or even walking half a mile with a full can of petrol. As for describing a funny noise to a monolingual Estonian mechanic... If I had a mechanical disaster I didn't know how to deal with, I wanted to know a man who did - and preferably one who spoke English.

He was hard to find. The proposed transit of the Baltic states eliminated the major organisations. I could just take the risk on those, perhaps; but Sod's Law would dictate that the cracked radiator, the blocked petrol feed would hold out into a few yards over the Lithuanian border before exploding. Eventually I found a satisfactory policy that wasn't impossibly expensive, and crossed one more item off the list.

One potential problem remained insoluble. If the van broke down on the motorway, there was a roughly even chance of doing so where the walk to a telephone and back could be beyond my range. Tough; I'd manage somehow, and anyway it wouldn't happen. Correct; it didn't.

So much for the plans, the superficial preparations. Now the time had come to commit myself.

CHAPTER II: SLINGS AND ARROWS

Hear me, auld Hangie, for a wee,

And let poor damned bodies be;

I'm sure sma' pleasure it can gie

E'en to a deil

To skelp and scaud poor dogs like me,

And hear us squeel!

(Burns: Address to the Deil)

Early February: time to initiate the hunt for a second-hand van.

After a few weeks' homework in the Midland Automart, I felt about as clued up as I ever would be about mileage and age versus price, and took the plunge with a three-year-old that had 30,000 miles on the clock. It was white with a chic brown stripe, and seduced me with the charms of its radio and stereo system.

As for the state of its insides, in my total ignorance I didn't even pretend to look. I settled for the obvious genuineness of the owner - and his written warranty that he was selling in good faith. I also mentioned in passing that my boyfriend was an Army mechanic; hoping to give the vendor the impression that Mike would be over to give him an oil and grease if there were any trickery. Unnecessary; the van proved an excellent buy.

Driving it home, though, I seriously wondered if I'd made the right decision. After the Escort, it felt about as sharp as a moped. Even on the motorway, it was hard to get the speed much above fifty. Was I really expecting to cover several thousand miles at this rate?

Perhaps there was a headwind that day. In any case, the little van seemed to speed up on better acquaintance. It was certainly nippy around town, and its list to the outside on whizzing round corners was positively exhilarating.

Small enough to wriggle into the least parking space, it was a gallon in a pint pot. The tiny engine had more oomph than I'd ever have believed; while subsequently, some frightful roads gave quite a battering to the vehicle, without breaking it down. In a very short time I was an ardent champion of the Rascal.

Inevitably, there were a few teething troubles. The horn didn't work; but only, as I found, because it was choked with cigarette ash. The seat belt took hold like a rottweiler, the jaws of its inertia mechanism having to be prised open before it would let go. And the choke button wouldn't stay out; the moment the van rolled forward, the socket slurped it back in, causing a jarring halt which would have redesigned my nose on the steering wheel... were my neck not clamped to the back of the seat by the vicious belt.

As always, the simplest cures were the best. A collar of blue-tac fixed the choke, while a clothes peg at the shoulder gave a bit of play to the belt and let me breathe.

Generally, the van hadn't been well maintained. It seemed a wise precaution to invest in a service and thorough going-over, before setting out, at a big specialist garage rather than going to my usual little workshop down the road. This would, no doubt, cost an arm and a leg, but at least I could be confident that it would be meticulously serviced and checked out by experts in the type. The first assumption, at least, was right.

Afterwards, checking over a couple of weeks, I was horrified to record under 30mpg. This was far short of what the Rascal was supposed to do, and would add telephone numbers to my estimated fuel costs. I took the van straight back to the garage, explaining the problem and the reason for my concern.

After an hour, one of the service managers came to the waiting room. Shifting from one foot to the other and faintly pink, he launched into a long obfuscating discourse on the nature of sparking plugs. It was only after some minutes, and then only because I was marginally less dim than he supposed, that the penny dropped: during several hundred pounds-worth of work, including a major service, they had forgotten to change the plugs - something even I could have done.

Now thoroughly red, he assured me there would be no further charge. He was fortunate that this wasn't one of my better days. With a brain like cold rice pudding and barely able to focus on his face, I couldn't manage to tell him where to put his plugs. I just took the keys wordlessly and tottered off home to bed and oblivion.

Yet this wasn't the end of the saga. After another fortnight, the figure had inched up to 31: still disastrous. Pessimistically, I rang the same garage yet again. Why, they asked, was I dissatisfied? Who had led me to expect better?

"Your own guru."

"Er... "

"Can you fetch him?"

Funnily enough, he was nowhere to be found. Meanwhile, a quick poll round the workshop produced a unanimous opinion that 31 was "brilliant for a Rascal". They were poor ambassadors for their splendid creature.

No help there; so I rang Vauxhall/Bedford HQ to ask what sort of faults might produce high petrol consumption? The engineers were unavailable at present, said the receptionist. She would call me back. She didn't.

Departure time was by now getting very close. I went to my little workshop down the road. The tickover was set a bit high, said the mechanic; not much, but he would adjust it. The figure went up from 31 empty to 34.5 laden, and I was well pleased.

It wouldn't be fair to leave this episode without a mention in dispatches for the spares salesman at the first garage. In going out of his way to drop an extra fanbelt literally on my doorstep, he earned my gratitude and respect; and restored my faith a little in large institutions.

*

I quickly found a buyer for the Ford. He was a very nice man who knew little more about cars than I did, and took me at my word as to its condition. But it was his bad luck that he arrived, without his cheque book, just as I had to go away for a week. Fortunately he was understanding, and agreed to pick up the car as soon as I was home again.

With less than a month before departure, it wasn't the wisest decision to spend a week at a cottage with no communications in a remote part of Wales. But I had committed myself to it back before last Christmas, and couldn't let my friends down.

I quelled my uneasiness with the thought that I could do with a rest away from the ever-growing files. In any case, I was well ahead with preparations, and could spare the time. This was arrant hubris, and the gremlins justly sniggered.

But it wasn't entirely wasted time. I managed to obtain my EU health form from a slate-built post office in a village with an unpronounceable name. I also finished the German novel, with triumph equalled only by relief, while my friends were walking in the hills. Meanwhile, I tried not to think about the remaining paperwork, and prayed the video was properly set to record the Cheltenham Gold Cup.

On the journey home, I stopped to phone the buyer of the Escort. By now very reasonably champing at the bit, he would be round at our own ETA plus one minute.

We arrived home and pulled up beside the car, to be confronted by a double whammie. After the test run itself, I'd managed to leave the lights on, and the battery was terminally ill. Worse, I'd reversed back in over a piece of glass. Flat battery, flat tyre, plus buyer arriving any minute, equalled flat spin.

I fetched the jump leads, while Mike sprinted for the footpump. After a couple of puffs the pump, capturing the mood of the moment, fell apart. The jump leads were more successful, and I sat revving furiously while Mike moved his car to an innocent distance and hid the leads in the boot. When my punter arrived moments later, the status quo was restored to the battery even if the tyre was only still half inflated: not quite a victory, but my public integrity at least patched up and tottering back on to its feet.

I explained about the slow puncture and gave him a tenner back for patch and glue, and he drove away satisfied in search of a garage with an air pump. We, meanwhile, staggered inside and reached for the gin bottle.

*

Almost immediately, a far more serious problem loomed.

A few weeks earlier, Mike had suspected lumps in a vital part of his anatomy. The doctor was soothing, but referred him to a specialist to be on the safe side. Now, to a casual enquiry about the state of play, Mike answered that both were growing.

It sounded bad. And to go swanning off round Europe if he were indeed condemned to the surgeon's knife was unthinkable. Preparations went on ice. With the exception of a few letters, I was arriving at the stage where most remaining arrangements had to be paid for - ferry tickets, Green Card, personal insurance and such things as wouldn't be recoverable on cancellation. The trip was financed out of my "retirement" gratuity. I couldn't afford to pay for it twice.

If, however, Mike were given the all-clear, I would still have a week and a half to tie up these loose ends. That, I thought comfortably, should be plenty of time. More hubris.

As the all-important date for the specialist drew near, Mike became increasingly tense and depressed. He had prepared himself for the worst, and was convinced that in a few weeks' time he would be eligible for the solo in Allegri's "Miserere".

The appointment was a long two hours' drive away. The journey passed in virtual silence, our occasional forced words dropping sullenly, without bouncing, like bricks. Although half-an-hour early, Mike was called almost at once, with a promptness that was half relief and half sentence. Ashen-faced, he walked slowly from the waiting room.

Twenty minutes later he was back, still ashen-faced. "What did he say?" I asked hoarsely.

"He said I'd got as healthy a pair there as he had ever seen."

It was All Systems Go.

*

Early next morning, I got to work.

The first thing was to confirm the Harwich-Hamburg return ferry and the Helsinki connection. To be sure of making the latter, it was essential to pre-book also the crossing from Estonia to Finland. No British travel agent dealt with this route, so I had to paddle my own canoe. Come to think of it, any mistakes, and I might be doing just that.

The Helsinki office looked more promising than Tallinn. I hoped fervently that someone at the other end could speak good English. If not, it would be a horrendously expensive waste of time trying to find common ground for communication, while the minutes ticked away inexorably at peak international rates.

No worries; even the answerphone was bilingual. I am now well drilled in the Finnish for: "Sorry; you are still on hold." The kind lady said it twenty-three times, so that I could get it right. But when I did eventually get through to Nikki at the sharp end, her English was better than mine, and I was fixed up in seconds. She sent a bubblingly cheerful letter confirming the reservation, and agreed to leave the ticket at the Tallinn office, rather than trusting it to the post with so little time left.

Next stop, car insurance and all-important Green Card. I had fondly imagined this to have been fully dealt with in February, for on switching my cover to the new van I had explained my future plans. That was the right time to ask that the policy, due to expire anyway at the end of March, might be replaced with one which would cover me throughout Europe.

The first early warning signal sounded on the expiry day itself. A letter arrived bearing glad tidings that the new policy, signed and sealed a month before, had been refused on the grounds of ME. This was an unexpected blow. My illness had occasionally raised queries in the past, but they were always solved by the doctor's certificate of roadworthiness: my own personal M.O.T. Now, however, it was a flat refusal. As far as they were concerned, I was unclean.

That was the bad news; the good was that another company would step into the void.... at 50% above the previous quote. Great. I binned the letter; then

15

on second thoughts fished it out, filed it, and started phoning.

It quickly emerged that if ME wasn't the flavour of the week, then vans were, for some reason, untouchable. Finally - at literally the last chance - I found a broker who could cover me with an affordable policy. Yes, all their policies automatically covered Europe, and provided a Green Card at no extra charge. Was he quite sure? Absolutely. We exchanged forms, and I ticked off one more item.

At last I began to relax. All the vital paperwork was now complete - at any rate, as far as I was concerned. All that remained was for office wheels to churn and the postman to deliver the goods.

Again, I couldn't have been more mistaken.

*

Plan A had been that I should be packed and ready at least a week before the game was afoot, leaving time to go into serious training for the off. Not, that is, with ten mile runs and rowing machines. I needed a week in bed, to build up a head of steam and ensure that, to start with at least, I was in some degree of working order. Now things were behind schedule, but there was no reason why there shouldn't be three or four days to spare.

Most remaining tasks concerned domestic arrangements. Bills first: gas, electricity, water and phone would all fall due while I was away and must be sorted out in advance. Then there were the animals. My old event horse Tim, now twenty-four, would be looked after jointly by Jan, owner of his three companions, and Trina, who has helped me every winter since illness struck. He was in good hands. For Nim, the resident Fat Cat, I left a timed two-day feeder, a huge pile of tins and minutely nit-picking instructions for the four people who had kindly agreed a rota for food and the occasional cuddle. Neal, who has taken charge of my garden for the last few years, promised to tackle the triffids at regular intervals.

Meanwhile Mike tackled the van, making a bed-frame from plywood and metal bars rescued from the scrap-heap at work. He was amused at my self-indulgent, four-inch foam slab that went on top; but I was going to be spending two-thirds of my life on that mattress for the next two months, and had no intention of roughing it. A kettle followed, a single burner gas stove... and of course the bucket. A couple of curtains fore and aft made from old material dug out of the loft, and the transformation from utility van to luxury motor caravan was complete. I only hoped that it wouldn't turn back to a pumpkin before I was home.

*

At the beginning of zero week, the Plagues of Israel erupted and the land brought forth frogs.

The softener arrived on Monday morning, in the shape of a water bill for the stables claiming a six-month consumption figure in excess of the last ten years' total. It was dated three weeks previously; yet despite its clear message of major problems, not to mention my own letter about imminent departure, the Water Board had kindly held on to it until the last possible moment.

Either there was a colossal leak, or it was vandalism. I bolted up to the field - five miles from home - and put a lock on the tap. Home again, I rang the accounts office and explained the circumstances. They would, said the sympathetic voice at the other end, send someone out urgently to check for a leak. Since this was also the morning on which I had discovered the van's latest frightful mileage figures, I was only too grateful to leave the ball in their court.

On the following morning the real bombshell fell, courtesy of my new insurance company. It wasn't the Green Card that dropped through the letterbox; rather, the joyful news that, despite their earlier assurance, they wouldn't cover me at all for the Czech Republic, Slovakia, Lithuania, Latvia or Estonia and, incidentally, they'd have an extra £60 for Poland, thankyou.

I was on the phone before I'd reached the bottom of the page. The person I'd spoken to before wasn't available; in fact, they didn't seem to know his name. Hardly surprising. No, there was no mistake - not this time, anyway - and the catastrophe was real.

Back to the original brokers. No help there; they didn't believe in eastern Europe either. Eventually, on Wednesday morning, I found an excellent firm specialising in Eastern Europe and the CIS, who would fill the gaps at a very reasonable price. Moreover, they could fax the application form to Mike's office, so that I could have it that evening.

Next to the Water Board, both Accounts and Depot, who for all their promises were displaying all the urgency of a drunken snail, having done precisely nothing; to Insurance Company no. 2, who had assured me they would send the now amended Green Card first class, and hadn't; to the local garage for new tyres and further consultations on petrol consumption; and a two-hour flit to Gloucester for my mattress. Far from building up, I was eating heavily into my basic daily rest. If I succeeded in going anywhere at all, it would be in a state of collapse.

Mike arrived, having left work well after five: no fax. He nobly went back in at nine-thirty, and came back bearing it triumphantly. I hadn't the heart to tell him it was no good: the secretary had sent only the top sheet of the proposal form and forgotten the all-important questionnaire. Moreover, Mike was away on a course the next day, so his fax machine wasn't available to me any more.

Thursday morning. The first Green Card was on the doormat. This was a good omen: real, live cover for three of my nine countries. After a rather irritable call to Insurance Company no.3, I was on my way to the nearest commercial fax office. One more hour, and formalities were completed. Tomorrow was Good Friday; one more post before I left on Saturday. I hoped desperately that the Post Office would do its stuff.

No chance to sit and gibber with relief or apprehension; time to ring the Water Board again and see if we could compromise on their definition of "urgency." But of course. They were sending out the cavalry; they'd be there the week after next. What did I say? Oh, well, I'd better turn the water off at the meter, then, until I got back, or at least until they had stirred themselves to take a look.

Staying vertical just long enough to arrange the loan of Neal's muscles to lift the heavy inspection cover, I fell into bed and stayed there for twenty-four hours.

On Friday, water duly off, I rang Jan and Trina. They were predictably delighted to learn that, for two months, watering the horses would mean lifting an enormous lump of metal and lying on their faces in the road to reach down to the tap. And with that, but for the comparatively trivial matter of packing the van, everything was under control.

*

Saturday morning: D-Day. The second Green Card was on the doormat, and even the sun managed to shine.

There had been no sense of pleasurable anticipation during the panics and disasters of the last week, and I felt strangely cheated. I had been literally dreading today, for fear that my plans would collapse, rather than looking forward to it in a state of leisurely excitement. As I climbed behind the wheel, still faintly frothing at the mouth, I was only just now believing in the reality of departure.

"Don't forget," said Mike, "if you do any damage to that van, I'll shrink you to a heap the size of a pea!"

Heartening words; and with them, I was off.

*

There had been no time to look out a route to the east coast. I tried a new one, and it was horribly slow. With the bare minimum of afternoon break, I was an hour late at my cousin's house at Frinton, on the Essex coast. Worse, when I got there, a strange rasping noise seemed to be coming from the van. But Chris and Sue feasted me royally, and I tried not to think of the coming weeks' baked beans waiting in the food box.

Next morning, I woke up to the sight of the Greensward and the sea, and the world wore a kindlier face. I was still reeling from the speed of my going; but these friendly signs, with their memories of carefree childhood holidays, smoothed out some of the furrows on my cheeks. Until now, everything possible had gone wrong. Now, it was time for the tide to turn.

Obligingly, it began at once. Chris tackled the Funny Noise, announcing within moments that I had left the radio on, untuned. The egg on my face tasted sweet: better a pillock than a pedestrian.

It was a late start, for the boat sailed at three. The pressure was off. The Gates were closed for a train, so I took a potter down the Greensward and around the little town for Auld Lang Syne. It was a lovely drive to Harwich on a minor road winding around salt-flat and estuary. The hedgerows were full of primroses and the first oil-seed rape was coming into early flower; a yellow land.

There was a long delay at the quay; the tiny van was lined up self-consciously along with monster motor caravans and commercial vehicles, and stood for an hour until the last car had gone on board. I fumed at first: could have had an extra hour in bed! But the delay was invaluable to reorganise luggage, flung in without due care and attention the previous day. When I was finally beckoned on everything was, appropriately, ship-shape.

The ferry was, as the brochure promised, luxurious, but (to me) rather alien territory. Space invaders, cinema and casino, restaurant meal £25; stingily, I decamped to the van for a brew. There was also - Hallelujah - a lift. Just as well, as the Plebs' accommodation was six flights of stairs below the main deck. The economy couchettes were of a size that an estate agent would describe as "cosy". No problem; six feet was all I needed. I bargained with my fellow travellers for a bottom bunk, since I would be spending a lot of time in it. No need for an explanation, as their immediately understanding sympathy showed they thought me a martyr to sea-sickness.

But the swaying motion of the boat was confusing, being just like the sensation of floating movement regularly produced by ME in the last stages before meltdown. Emerging from my bed that evening I felt something subconsciously puzzling me. It took some minutes before the penny dropped: I was feeling rested, so why was the floor still going up and down?

Twenty-four hours horizontal did much to patch over the ravages of the last few days. When I finally staggered upstairs, blinking in the sunlight, the North Sea was behind and the banks of the Elbe were rapidly sliding past.

HAMBURG

POLAND

BERLIN

GERMANY

DRESDEN
Königstein
Erzgebirge

•Nelahozeves
PRAGUE   • Pardubice

CZECH
REPUBLIC

•Sloup
BRNO • •Slavkov

SLOVAKIA

AUSTRIA   • BRATISLAVA

Györ •

HUNGARY

CHAPTER III: DON'T... MENTION... THE WAR!

In England, Walls make ice cream.

(Graffito on the Berlin Wall)

Hamburg passed in a blur. I struggled with driving on the right, with unfamiliar road markings, with continental traffic lights hiding up lamp-posts. Somehow the Berlin motorway contrived to pop up directly ahead, and before I knew it I was out in open country and burning up the miles.

This was flat, drab landscape. Much was wooded; but even the pines and birch trees were uniformly sized and spaced, with Germanic precision. Occasional lengths of five-foot wire kept back the deer, but more often even the motorway was open to the surrounding countryside, which itself had only barely heard of Enclosure. Most Europeans seem to lack the urge to make boundaries, that blind compulsion which led some of our own more northerly forebears to drive stone walls up sheer mountainsides, just for the hell of it.

The road was busy, and the little van even managed to pass a couple of other vehicles. Closer to Berlin, however, the traffic became choked. It seemed the ideal point to pull off for my compulsory afternoon stop.

But by late afternoon, the snarl-up was even worse. This was the evening of Easter Monday; it wasn't going to improve. Another few miles at the crawl, and I decided to leave the motorway and try out rural Germany earlier than I'd intended. It was an interesting diversion, giving an immediate insight into the poverty of the former East Germany. The villages on the way reminded me of the news reports coming out of Romania or Albania in recent years; drab, ramshackle buildings badly maintained, few vehicles, cobbled streets. The first time I hit cobbles I thought them rather quaint, until I realised that the road meant to stay this way at least until the next village, fifteen miles further. It was depressing; I hadn't bargained for such austerity until the wilder parts of Poland or the Baltic states. At least it was more scenic than the motorway, and at 20mph there was ample time to enjoy the view.

Back on a main road, I thankfully put my foot down. Thirty miles out from Berlin, though, the traffic jams returned, putting paid to any remaining chance of getting there in daylight.

A maze of deserted buildings behind a high wire fence lined the last few miles of road. They were mostly pre-fabs and apartment blocks, with here and there an old, decaying manor house. Trees grew right up to the walls, almost hiding them; boards covered their windows. They appeared to have been barracks. Signs warned of *lebensgefahr*, but whether from homicidal guards or just falling debris wasn't clear. A hang-out of Erich Honecker's Merry Men, perhaps. Already a picture of life behind the Iron Curtain was gaining substance.

I'd planned to arrive in the early evening, with time to find my way around the city in the van before dusk; the ground I could cover on foot would necessarily be limited. Now it was almost dark.

But this was Berlin, and I had been waiting years for this moment. To go tamely straight to bed was unthinkable. I could at least find my bearings, and, in the process, somewhere to stop overnight.

I came into the centre via the Kurfürstendamm, Europe's glitziest street for shopping and restaurants. Now illuminated in a kaleidoscope of neon lights, it surely looked better by night anyway. I continued in style via the Siegessäule, or Victory Column, a two-hundred foot monument to the Franco-Prussian Wars. From here the road ran as straight as an arrow between the lawns and parks of the Tiergarten and right up to the Brandenburg Gate, still half a mile away but already dominating the view.

For thirty years the Gate was diminished by the Berlin Wall, running right beneath it. Now all was as if the concrete and barbed-wire monstrosity had never existed; while the only searchlights were those trained on the Gate itself, in celebration rather than threat. A short wiggle past, and the road continued into the former Eastern Sector along Unter den Linden, whose embassies, hotels and restaurants once formed the heart of Imperial Berlin.

Beyond, a nightmare of busy roads caught me unawares, and I made an unintentional rundfahrt of several miles before extricating myself and regaining the Brandenburg Gate. Although only a couple of hundred yards away, the Reichstag was by contrast quiet and deserted. Here, free of the threatening traffic, I could at last stop and take stock of the impressions that had been hurtling at me from all directions over the last half-hour.

Built over a century ago to house the Parliament of the newly established German Federal Empire, the Reichstag was seriously damaged when it was fired by anarchists in 1933, four weeks after the Nazis came to power. Hitler publicly blamed the Communist Party for the destruction, siezing the occasion to take measures against them. Tonight, it wasn't hard to imagine the friendly yellow of the spotlights replaced by the red glow of fire, and picture the inferno as it burned.

But there was no more time for such self-indulgence. I needed food, and somewhere to sleep. My luck was in, for skirting the car park to the rear I spotted several camper vans, obviously there to stay. Apparently, the authorities turned a blind eye to overnight parking this early in the year.

Room for one more. I mentally reserved a spot for the night, before returning to the Kurfürstendamm, where I had promised myself supper to celebrate the real beginning to the trip. But parking was difficult, the multiplicity of restaurants confusing, and my legs on strike.

And so dinner on the Kurfürstendamm on my first night in Berlin was a takeaway from Burger King.

*

Next morning, daylight awarded five stars to my campsite. Across the River Spree, on the other side of some wasteland, was a long stretch of the Wall. While I watched, a train thundered contemptuously over the top on a track raised high above it, without even slackening speed.

To my generation it feels as if there never was a time before the Berlin Wall existed, so deeply did it become entrenched in the collective consciousness of the West. It seemed as aboriginal as the Big Bang. Yet in actual fact it stood for less than thirty years.

It was on the 13th August 1961 that Berliners woke up to find their city split by a barrier of barbed wire, thrown up overnight, and quickly strengthened with a brick and block construction. Cynically labelled the "Anti-Fascist Protection Wall", it was built against the rising tide of escapees to the West, via the Allies' enclave of West Berlin.

The prototypes were replaced over the next couple of years with the final model, complete with regular watchtowers and the infamous "Deathstrip" - fifty metres of floodlit, heavily guarded open space on the eastern side. It lasted intact until the "Velvet Revolution" of autumn 1989, when the gathering momentum of pro-democracy movements throughout eastern Europe sent Communist governments toppling like dominoes. As they passed into history, the Wall followed hard on their heels.

I was surprised that some of it still stood; most had fallen to demolition firms, souvenir hunters - and entrepreneurs selling bits off it. Mentally adding another item to my list for the day, I set out to explore.

By day, the difference in "East" Berlin was obvious; drab, utilitarian buildings here and there spruced up, perhaps by western firms, elsewhere crumbling or breaking out in a rash of scaffolding. The famous Linden trees were still disappointingly in their winter plumage. Throughout the city, spring was a good month behind that which I had left at home.

The Brandenburg Gate, however, takes your breath away at any time of year. This triumphal monument was commissioned by the Emperor Friedrich Wilhelm II and completed in 1791. No longer emasculated by the proximity of the Wall, it is now once again a focal point for the the newly re-united city.

It is modelled on the entry gate to the Acropolis of Athens, with its massive structure softened by neo-classical reliefs. Panels in the columns celebrate the eternal human diversions of feasting, fighting and hunting, while along the pediment Lapiths and Centaurs find a score of different ways to club each other to death.

Above its Doric columns is the Quadriga, a statue of Victory enthroned in a chariot. This has enjoyed a chequered life. Taken home by Napoleon as a souvenir in 1806, it was won back like a sporting trophy eight years later. It was heavily restored after bomb damage in the second War; and temporarily removed again in 1989 after Berliners, ecstatic at the collapse of the Wall, climbed right over the Gate and accidentally knocked bits off it.

Although a thoroughfare once again, the Gate is closed to all traffic except taxis and buses, making life easier for visitors on foot. Tourists congregate in the Pariser Platz on the east side. Here among the bus-stops and taxi ranks are the usual souvenir stalls, selling Russian and East German army caps, medals and badges, as well as *matroshkas*, or Russian dolls.

Only a couple of hundred yards to the south is a more sinister place, the Potsdamer Platz. It was from his bunker somewhere here that Hitler directed the closing stages of the War, and here also that the partly burned body was found after his eventual suicide. The actual spot is a closely guarded secret, for fear of its becoming a Neo-Nazi shrine.

From here I caught a bus to the television tower, whose thousand-foot altitude must give a spectacular view of the city. There were "long delays due to technical problems", and the queue stretched right down into the square outside. Never mind; the day was hazy and I probably wouldn't have seen much anyway. I abandoned the idea, consoling myself with hot chocolate from the street vendor outside - real, thick liquid chocolate the like of which I haven't tasted before.

It kept me going all the way to the Nikolaiviertel, the district surrounding St. Nikolai's Church. At first sight, this looked like a real, unspoiled quarter of old Berlin; it came as a shock to discover that it is a fake, conceived after the forms of specific earlier buildings, and built over bombsites by post-war Communist architects better schooled in concrete and breeze block.

Little of Berlin came through the war even partly unscathed. The Church itself, the height of its twin towers exaggerated by the narrow streets, was heavily damaged, although not entirely rased. Before its reconstructed façade, two pseudo-mediaeval buskers playing real mediaeval music on bagpipe and tabor were convincing actors on a well-constructed stage.

Fifty years on, it is still impossible to escape World War Two here. On the way to the tube station stood the remains of a once-impressive Franciscan Monastery, with a plaque on the wall telling of its destruction by Allied bombing. I found the various aspects of the political aftermath of war commemorated in the Checkpoint Charlie Museum, which chronicled the segregation of East and West, and celebrated the whole eastern European freedom movement in annotated photographs and a video show. These began with the gloom of the Hungarian Uprising and the Soviet invasion following the Prague Spring, continued through the rise of Solidarity and reached a triumphant conclusion with the Velvet Revolution. The museum exhibits included the microlite glider which carried a young Czech and his small son over the Wall, and a radiogram in which a girl was concealed and smuggled to the West.

By the time I had left the museum, my four hours' ration was up; any longer, and I would be into Extra Time. But I couldn't give up without a closer look at the Wall. Finding my way to the river bank opposite the Reichstag, I drove along a stretch of wasteland which in former times was part of the Deathstrip. Some two hundred yards of Wall remained, decorated from end to end with sombre black paintings commenting on its history. At one end an In Memoriam section numbered each year's dead.

Nearby stood a crumbling concrete watchtower, lengths of rusty barbed wire trailing in dejection and shame from its top. Three gutted and abandoned tanks reared in a mock trilithon, gaudily painted with flowers and whorls by some irreverent artist.

By now I was starving with the unaccustomed exercise, and would have sold my soul for a bar of chocolate. Back at the Reichstag carpark, I lunched off a whole tin of stew, and was still hungry.

*

You couldn't miss the funfair. Raucous music thundered in conflicting keys from tens of rides and hundreds of stalls; while a fifty-foot mechanical King

Kong guarded the entrance, waving his metal arms wildly and croaking sinister, gutteral threats.

I hesitated longingly by the water splash; but people were emerging damp or worse, and the evening was chilly. So I opted for a ride on the big wheel, the largest moveable one, it was claimed, in the world. "Alleen?" said the attendant in the Berlin dialect, and I had to ask him to repeat himself. From the top, the view of night-time Berlin was breathtaking, and more than made up for the TV Tower disappointment.

Afterwards, I found a real loo, then supped off chips and chocolate-soaked pancakes; and reckoned the evening an unqualified success.

*

I slept long and deeply, waking relaxed and, after the excitements of the previous day, content for once to stay longer in bed. It was a welcome relief from the suffocating blend of fidgety impatience with physical catalepsy which usually starts my day.

It wasn't, however, peaceful. A motor-bike instructor was using the quiet park as a suitable place to train a succession of pupils. Corpulent, moustached like the Kaiser and the embodiment of Prussian precision, he stood at one end supervising as they repeated his drill endlessly and without variation: away, turn, return, over and over until they, I, and surely he, were sick of it.

Worse, under such constant vigilance there was no chance to empty my bucket.

I decided on a stratagem of opening the van door, quickly throwing the bucket contents at the nearby drain as if it were innocent washing-up water, and driving off rapidly before anyone noticed the difference. It was bad luck that the Kaiser chose this time to switch ends. I had whipped back the door and swung my arm before I saw him; and watched appalled as the stream sliced through the air, glinting cheerily in the sun, and landed with a splatter somewhere near his feet. In less than a second I was in the front seat and screaming out of the park as if the entire Prussian cavalry were at my heels.

Today, I planned to drive about the city and stop off at various points. After yesterday I couldn't reckon on doing much walking. I began with the Tiergarten, once a hunting ground of woodland and swamp providing deer and boar for Imperial amusement; now tamed, mown and planted with acres of spring bulbs. Under the trees, thickly growing chionodoxa looked from a distance like bluebells. For half an hour I lazed, breathed, enjoyed and generally finished waking up. I couldn't, however, walk far enough to escape the roar of the traffic. So I rejoined it and headed back past the Brandenburg Gate towards the Pergamum Museum.

This was a must, for it housed - indeed was built, and named for - the top (more interesting) half of the Temple of Apollo from Pergamum. Years before, I had visited the bottom half, left behind in Turkey.

But when I reached the museum, building work blocked the path. My legs, aching from the day before, didn't care for three sides of a square. Reluctantly I cancelled the Temple, had a look at the nearby Cathedral instead, then returned thankfully to my wheels and quitted central Berlin in the direction of the Schloss Charlottenburg.

Built by the Elector Friedrich in 1695 for his Queen Sophie Charlotte, the Charlottenburg Palace acquired this name only after her death. Subsequently a favourite summer residence for the Kings of Prussia, it is today a museum.

Its creamy-white, red-roofed façade surrounds on three sides the entrance courtyard, where a statue of Sophie Charlotte's father-in-law, the Great Elector Friedrich-Wilhelm, glowers at visitors. Perhaps he is daring you to remind him that he spent the war at the bottom of a nearby lake for safe-keeping.

To either side of the Schloss, enormous wings stretch for a hundred yards in each direction. Behind it, gardens reaching down to a bend in the River Spree are said to resemble the landscaped park of an English country house.

Too far for me today; content merely to look from a distance, I wandered a little way into the courtyard and sat on the wall in glorious April sunshine. The main Brandenburg road, only a hundred yards behind, might not have existed, its dust and noise screened by a belt of trees. I was in no hurry to rejoin it.

*

There was one more place I wanted to visit before leaving Berlin.

A short hop from the main road, beyond an area of high-rise flats and wooded parks, was the Olympic Stadium built for the Berlin Games in 1936. The city was pressing hard to be awarded the Millennium Games, and in the car park flew a line of "Olympic 2000" flags.

Inside, the stadium had undergone changes since those early days of excitement. The cinder running track had long since been replaced by tartan, and the stands built high and covered, to hold many thousands more spectators. Today it was silent, almost deserted; yet it felt complacent with past glories, as if a sort of vibrant thrill had soaked into its fabric.

Hitler's '36 Games were intended as a showpiece of Aryan supremacy, an advertisement to the world of the vigour throbbing throughout the Third Reich from the personal to the National level. But things did not go quite according to plan when the black athlete Jesse Owens walked away with four gold medals. Only a few yards from where I stood now, the Führer had sat grinding his teeth while the "Untermensch" outran the best of German manhood.

Back outside, a Japanese runner had just arrived at the entrance with a flaming torch. Either he was several years early, or perhaps he was just a publicity stunt. I didn't wait to find out, as time was getting on and the road was calling.

First, I found a supermarket where I stocked up on bread, chocolate, apples, chocolate, coke and chocolate. Immediately next door a was garage, where, in apology for the rubbish that was probably coming later, I filled the van with the most expensive "Super Bleifrei".

Then it was back into the traffic to find the Dresden road. And what traffic! My final memories of Berlin will be forever linked with petrol fumes and first gear. The tangle was largely due to the German government's heroic attempt to update the infrastructure of the former East. But it took an hour to get out, and I was running very late when I stopped for my break.

The eighty remaining miles to Dresden were over frightful road surface, and I feared for my shock-absorbers - not to mention the van's. Here, too, valiant efforts were in hand to improve the road, but so far only on the other carriageway. The inference was inescapable: anyone going east deserved all they got.

I could have done with a smooth ride. Yesterday's mileage was catching up. The old ache in my chest was back, so that I wanted to draw up my legs and hunch over the wheel, and my sight was beginning to blur. For inspiration, I burrowed in the tape box. This was the fringe of J.S.Bach country, and I found a Prelude & Fugue on the tape of one of my father's organ recitals.

There could be nothing more energising than the magnificent reeds of the Hereford Cathedral organ, especially when some rousing Walton followed the Bach. I turned the volume up and bounced over the potholes at least 5mph faster, and was swept into Dresden on the tidal wave of Crown Imperial.

There couldn't have been a more appropriate overture.

*

Dresden has been justly called the "Florence of the Elbe". Generations of architects have fashioned its local sandstone into Classical, Baroque and Neo-Renaissance elegance; its many art galleries represent most of Europe's most famous artists; while a number of great composers have lived and worked here.

Originally a Slav fishing village, its early name "Drezgajan" meant "people of the forest". The nearby Erzgebirge - "Ore Mountains" - gave it wealth in the form of silver, later gold and other precious metals and stones. By the thirteenth century it was a sizeable city, and became the seat of the Dukes, afterwards Kings, of Saxony. Briefly, in the time of Duke Augustus the Strong, Poland was ruled from Dresden.

Its prosperity vanished abruptly on the night of February 13th 1945, when saturation bombing reduced much of the city to rubble. The centre was mostly restored after the war, but bombsites remain to this day. A notable example is the Frauenkirche, Church of Our Lady, deliberately left in ruins as a reminder of the war. Its current restoration programme is both a focus and a symbol of Dresden's second renaissance in fifty years.

Dresden's welcome to a tired and disorientated motorist was not as forgiving as that of Berlin. Again I arrived later than planned, and unprepared for the nightmare new experience of tram-dodging in the dark on its cobbled roads. There was no friendly back-street carpark. I spent the night in a residential street, waking late, utterly drained, and resigned to a necessarily superficial view of the city.

I left the van in the Altmarkt, right under the tower of the Kreuzkirche. Inside the church, a photographic exhibition showed the horrific destruction of the bombing. Not a brick had escaped. Among heaps of debris only a few vertical piles of tottering stone still stood, with not a single piece of transverse brickwork remaining: charred stumps with no branches after a forest fire. My mind sprang to Beirut as the only comparable example of my lifetime, but this was worse, far worse.

To coincide with the exhibition, the tower was open to the public. What should have been a lucky chance gave me only colossal frustration, as it would have given a wonderful view over Dresden - if only I could have got up all the stairs.

But when I walked the streets, I realised that I hadn't missed much; the view would have been disappointing. For with the marks of war still clearly upon Dresden, it is only now, with the influx of western wealth, that much of the restoration is finally being completed. Moreover, fifty years of unchecked pollution have smeared the rooftops with grime, now being slowly scraped off. The skyline over much of Dresden's treasures is shaped by cranes and scaffolding.

Much of the Palace, for instance, was hidden under boards, loose bricks and cement dust. I skirted it by the Princes' Procession, under the lowering eyes of a couple of Visigoths, guarding a gateway in eight feet of sandstone. Outside the Cathedral I was stopped by a Croatian refugee begging for alms. She was something of a shock in surroundings such as these.

Inside, the Katholische Hofkirche was sumptuous in the extreme. It is said to be a Baroque masterpiece; but I found myself discomfited rather than awed by its abundance of gold ornament, cake-frill plaster and uninhibited, frolicking cherubs.

It was built for Augustus the Strong, who firmly believed that "Princes acquire immortality by what they build." To make doubly sure of his own he sired, by the official estimate, 365 children. His heart is buried here, in a bronze casket. They say that it flutters every time a pretty girl goes by.

Among his memorials Augustus commissioned the Zwinger Palace, also in flamboyantly Baroque style and modelled in part on the Grand Trianon at Versailles. But he didn't live there; the palace was reserved for court festivities and exhibitions. Today its galleries house some of the finest art treasures in Europe.

A narrow archway gave access to it from the square before the Opera House, opening on to a wide courtyard of lawns, gravelled walks and fountains, like a slightly sugary Oxford college. At its farther end stood the Kronentor, or Crown Gate. This was Augustus' tribute to himself on becoming King of Poland: an arched gateway surmounted by a copper crown bearing the letters ARP - Augustus, Rex Poloniae. Behind it, a bridge led over an unexpectedly business-like moat. With a shock, I found myself suddenly back in a busy street, a far cry from the narrow alleys of the old quarter.

On the further side of the Altmarkt I discovered the ruin of the Frauenkirche, now a hive of human and mechanical activity. For after fifty years of standing deep in its own rubble, it is now to be restored almost stone by stone from that same rubble. The project is ambitious, and, at an estimated DM160 million, expensive. Local opinion is divided.

On the one hand, the venture is seen as an almost ritual gesture, a final act of erasing the marks of the war and its aftermath. But there are many who would rather see the money spent on something of more immediate practical value, such as housing or industry. For Dresdeners are feeling the economic pinch as much as anywhere in eastern Germany, with many local factories forced to close for lack of the subsidies delivered under Communist rule.

The camera at my belt was an example. Made at a Dresden factory, it had cost three times as much to produce as I had actually paid for it in England, new. But the Praktica works, grossly overmanned, had been shut down almost before the ink was dry on the document of reunification.

Yet for all the uncertainties there is a sense of rebirth in Dresden, from the hum of its busy streets up to the creaks and bangs of machinery about its grime-blackened towers; a sense of the indestructible. For neither the horror of the Blitz nor the poverty of the Communist years were able to reduce it to mediocrity.

*

For all Dresden's treasures, I was ready to move on. For the moment I had had enough of the throb of big cities, with the associated motorways, traffic and crowds. Moreover, east or not, this was still Germany, and at least partly familiar; whereas the Czech Republic was completely unknown territory, and beckoning strongly.

Avoiding the main autoroute, I took the Pirna road which follows the River Elbe through the dramatic cliffs of the Elbe Sandstone mountains, known as the Saxon Switzerland. First, however, it passed through Dresden's industrial hinterland, with some the grim polluting factories I had been expecting to see in the former eastern bloc. Already much has been done to reduce pollution from eastern Germany's industry, but as in other things, progress is jerky, a thing of shreds and patches.

So was the juxtaposition of Skodas with Mercedes on the roads; there was little in between. Coming out of Pirna on to the first of the sandstone ridges, I followed a Trabant which blew out a thick cloud of smoke. The "Trabi", mainstay of East Germany's private transport, has a plastic body and a two-stroke engine. Utilitarian in the extreme, it is said to be able to run on a mixture of heating oil and kerosene, and even on petrol one Trabi produces more pollution than a hundred cars with catalytic convertors. As the one in front of me accelerated past a lorry, leaving me totally blinded inside a black cloud, I wasn't inclined to argue with the statistic.

Below me stretched the Elbe, still astonishingly broad so far upstream. On a ridge above it crouched the great castle of Königstein, once the property of the Saxon Dukes. I took a brief look at it from the car park, but there was an uphill walk to the castle itself; and my enthusiasm to go closer didn't survive the sight of the "Festungsexpress", a sort of motorised vehicle thinly disguised as a train and filled with hearty tourists and bawling children.

On the other hand Königstein village, dramatically sited right under the castle rock, was enchanting. It was almost alpine with its narrow cobbled streets, window boxes and fast-flowing stream. Many of the cottages were topped with curving Dutch-type gables under steep, red-tiled roofs. In the main street "Bogart's Bar", its window lined with pictures of the actor, looked oddly out of place.

The border town of Bad Schandau was similarly attractive. Squeezed between the cliffs and the river, it was graced by some beautiful old houses, their elegance in no way diminished by slightly crumbling, faded exteriors. In one of these I found the Post Office, and was able at last to buy stamps for my mounting pile of cards.

Almost before I knew it, I was at the border. A tall soldier in his mid-teens gave me a cheerful "Dobri Den!". It sounded exactly like Russian, which made me jump. I returned the greeting, at which conversation terminally foundered. After a few helpless gestures at his superior officer, he gave me a shrug of his shoulders, a charming smile and a wave through. And that was all. Here, at least, the Iron Curtain had rusted clean away.

CHAPTER IV: PRAGUE SPRING

Though the latitude's rather uncertain,

And the longitude also is vague,

The persons I pity who know not the city,

The beautiful city of Prague.

(William Jeffrey Prowse)

The Czech Republic introduced itself with an enigma. For the first few miles the road, still following the Elbe, ran gently but steadily downhill. Yet I was travelling upstream. Perhaps the glorious principles of Marxist-Leninism had been invoked to persuade the river to flow backwards.

Fortunately the guide book had warned me of the unfamiliar system of road marking: very few white lines, with a system of yellow lozenges indicating right of way or otherwise. It also warned of a hundred and one ways to collect on-the-spot fines. I would have to watch my P's & Q's, having already pushed my luck with one or two almighty blunders. But I had the stage to myself to rehearse on; the roads were almost entirely empty of traffic.

At first, some very pretty villages lay tucked between the uplands and the river. But gradually the hills fell away, and the countryside turned drab and industrial, the villages functional and rather decayed. Above them drooped the cats'-cradles of wires, hanging from not-quite-vertical and superfluous poles, that often characterise third-world countries. I was reminded of the more Europeanised parts of Turkey.

*

Morning arrived on a bleak upland somewhere above the confluence of the Elbe with the River Moldau. The weather was sunny but wintry, with the crops along the road only a few inches high and the trees tight-budded. The song of skylarks filled the air.

I was already very jaded. Each day so far had piled on its quota of exhaustion, like layers of extra-thick sweaters, making it difficult to move. It was a struggle to wash my hair in a thimbleful of water, with the cold wind thrusting knives into my every crevice. But I felt better for it as I climbed into the front seat and headed, vicariously, for Prague.

The little village of Nelahozeves, a dozen miles north-west of the capital, is the birthplace of the Czech Republic's most famous composer, Antonín Dvořák. From the crag above it glowers a rather gloomy chateau, decorated by garish wall-paintings. Today it was empty of life but for kestrels, nesting on windowsills and flying from crevices in the rock.

In the village below, I found a balding, rather cross-looking Dvořák conducting in marble at the centre of a small park alongside the house where he was born. This looked rather grand for Dvořák's family, who were innkeepers and butchers. The son was destined for the same career; but his skills on organ and violin earned him a place at the Prague Organ School, and the rest is history.

My second detour, for information and currency, was to Prague airport. This plan, easier than walking round town looking for a bank, was still something of a timewaster, and the morning was well on when I finally hit the city.

More terrible traffic; but it gave me leisure to appreciate the wide streets and elegant buildings. Here spring had arrived at last. The sticky buds had burst into tentative life on the many chestnut trees, while in the gardens forsythia and almond dripped blossom.

At the zoo car park, a cheery attendant gave me lots of useful advice on where to buy tickets for public transport and what change to get for the machines. I planned to leave the van here rather than fight a way through the traffic all day; anyway it was high time to ride on a tram. But there was another reason for picking just this spot to park.

For decades Prague Zoo has been at the forefront of breeding the Przewalski Horse. This ancient creature, drawn by Stone Age man in cave paintings 25,000 years ago, is the world's only truly wild, as opposed to feral (or escaped domestic), horse. Genetically different from all domestic breeds in the same way as are the donkey, zebra and other equids, it was "discovered" for the west in its (then) native Mongolia by the Russian explorer Colonel Nikolai Przewalski in 1878.

Twenty years later there was a frantic, competitive scramble to capture live specimens for the zoos and private collections of Europe. The method used was primitive in the extreme. Mares were shot to enable capture of their foals, which were then transported vast distances west by the new Trans-Siberian Railway.

Not surprisingly, many died, and in fact only thirteen both lived and produced descendants to this day. Yet, ironically, it was this savage campaign which ensured the survival of the breed. For around twenty-five years ago, after surviving millennia of hunting by man, the Przewalski Horse became extinct in the wild.

It may not remain so for long; a number of schemes are under way to re-introduce it to Mongolia. Already two groups were on Mongolian soil, awaiting release next year. I hoped to travel and see them in Mongolia in the future; for now I would meet them in captivity.

On the side of a hill overlooking the city and occupying gardens of deliciously scented shrubs, Prague Zoo was a pleasant place to while away an hour or so... for people, at any rate. On the other side of the wire, life was less idyllic for some of its inmates.

The path to the horses passed dismal tiny cages of various fox-like creatures. They displayed all the neuroses of too-closely confined captive animals, running endlessly back and forth and pausing only to wonder, with bright-eyed desperation, if I had a titbit. I hadn't, and they drooped mournfully for a second or two before resuming their mindless to and fro. I passed the remaining cages as fast as I could, eyes fixed straight ahead.

The Przewalskis, at least, had plenty of space. One of the elite exhibits, they enjoyed three large paddocks, the main one being for a "harem group" of a stallion and six mares.

They were a lively bunch, constantly letting off steam. The dust in the hilly, stony paddock had hardly settled when one or two would be off again, bickering and bullying; or because the lively yearlings next door had set them off; or sometimes spontaneously, just for the hell of it.

In between times they wandered restlessly, coming together, dispersing to the three corners of the triangular enclosure, returning to pick at their hay, but rarely still for long. Perhaps the steepness of their paddock, in keeping them fit, discouraged the lethargy you often see in zoo animals; or perhaps they are by nature more active than the domestic horse. Maybe one day I would watch them completely unconfined in Mongolia, and learn the answer.

*

With a double handful of tickets in my pocket, I hopped on a bus for the centre.

Prague is built on a pattern common to many central European capitals. The hub of temporal and spiritual power is vested in the citadel of Hradčany, which houses both castle and cathedral, while public activity centres on the

Town Square in the Old Quarter. Here, as elsewhere, I intended to use public transport to reach the highest point I wanted to visit. This meant that much of the subsequent legwork would be downhill, which could as much as double my range.

Unfortunately, although my legs were waking up, my brain was fogged with the over-enthusiasm of the last few days, which rather took the fun out of things. It also led to silly mistakes. At least by the time I reached the castle, having unnecessarily tried out bus, metro and four trams, I was a veteran of Prague's public transport. I gave five stars to the metro, for its speed, cleanliness... and generous provision of escalators. The trams, however, got the thumbs down. As they rattled over the bumpy lines, their lack of springs and hard plastic chairs chipped lumps off my seatbones.

Prague Castle turns out to be more château than castle, once you pass the outer fortifications. These include a gatehouse and bridge over a deep ditch on the north side, while the south is naturally guarded by a precipitous crag.

Inside I found a succession of rather featureless courtyards, blandly walled in plaster and granite. Then a short step under an archway brought me out in front of Hradčány's architectural raison d'être, the Gothic cathedral of St. Vitus.

Above the west door its twin towers soared almost out of sight, over a bewildering arrangement of pointed arches, needle-like pinnacles, and rows of flying buttresses marching down both sides. The interior was just as grand, its pillars rising to an enormous height under the vaulted roof, drawing the gaze along the nave to a long, thin triptych of stained glass beyond the altar.

Among the number of side chapels was one dedicated to St. Václav, better known as Wenceslas. Never really a king, he was actually a Duke of Bohemia, and an early Christian leader, who was deposed and murdered by his pagan brother, Boleslav the Cruel. It was Wenceslas, now patron saint of the Czech Republic, who built the first church on this site in 925 AD.

If his chapel is the finest, the tomb of St. John of Nepomuk, a local martyr, is the most memorable - if for the wrong reasons. A sugary pile covered entirely in silver, it is watched over by a quartet of silver cherubs capering above it on wires, like pantomime fairies.

Outside, it was difficult to appreciate fully either the scale or the beauty of the cathedral; so completely does it fill the courtyard that I could enjoy it only a little at a time. Perhaps its most striking feature was the the south entrance, the so-called Golden Gate, decorated with a mediaeval mosaic in which God sits enthroned in a scarlet cloud, giving judgement on a shuddering crowd of mortals. On the grille below, fashioned in exquisite detail, is a set of cameos of everyday peasant life: a reaper pausing to take a swig from a jug of ale, two farmers killing a pig, an old woman appropriately gathering winter fuel.

At the far end of the courtyard a narrow entry squeezed between the Royal Palace and St. George's Basilica, leading down to the creamy-white stones of the inaptly named Black Tower, which has guarded the eastern gate for nine centuries. Beyond was a cobbled lane, heading downhill at an alarming angle.

I stopped to rest in an embrasure, and found myself looking out over a breath-taking view. All Prague presented itself. Directly ahead were the narrow streets and tree-lined gardens of the Mala Strana, or Little Quarter; further, over the red gables of the Waldstein Palace, threaded the blue line of Prague's main artery, the River Vltava; while beyond, an anonymous tangle of roofs sheltered the Old Town. Away to the right was the citadel of Vyšehrad, site of one of the earliest Slav settlements.

Running the gauntlet of the trinket sellers on the castle steps, I stopped by a chip stand at the bottom. Very much the insular Brit; but I had a long way to go, and would run more efficiently on a lot of short rests with frequent injections of carbohydrate, than on the transiently full stomach of a proper lunch.

Cobbled lanes jostled the citadel's base. Walled gardens lined every street; from branches yet barely green, long fingers of blossom hung over the streets. Past the Malostranske Square, dodging the odd tram - I'd almost forgotten by now that they existed - and down to the Charles Bridge, where I found a pizza vendor, just in time for my next carbohydrate fix. I carried my lunch under the Gothic archway of Prague's oldest bridge, and sat on the parapet under St. Wenceslas's statue to eat at leisure.

It was a good vantage point. Standing, I could see the six-hundred-yard length of the bridge, and watch the multiplicity of buskers, artists, one-man-shows and performers of every description who, along with the street vendors, entertained the crowd. Very appropriate; where, after all, can you find Bohemians if not in Bohemia? I didn't even try to count the statues looking down with varying degrees of disapproval. Turning the other way, I could look down the arm of the Vltava called the Devil's Stream, as far as the great wooden water wheel of the former Grand Priory of the Knights of Malta. Here, stately old houses peer over the water from behind half-closed shutters, and steps lead down to the waterfront of what has become known as Little Venice.

At the western end of the Charles bridge is a single massive tower topped with more Gothic spires. To pass underneath is to cross from light to dark, from the sun and space of the river to the crowding shadow of the Old Town.

Above a labyrinth of narrow, winding streets, the bright sunlight of mid-afternoon slid down red tiles, squeezed between a multiformity of gables and ran out of steam barely halfway down the brightly coloured walls. It was hard to keep any sense of direction through the twists and turns, but somehow I emerged blinking into the sunlight of the Old Town Square.

A market place for a thousand years, this is still the hub of popular Prague, although the hucksters' stalls have long since given way to the tables and chairs of numerous cafés. Its limits are defined by the Town Hall at the eastern end, and the twin towers, blackened by the soot of centuries, of the Týn Church opposite. In stark contrast to both is St. Nicholas' Church, its white Baroque face topped by cheerful green domes and the inevitable red tiles. In front of all, centre stage, is the monument to Jan Hus.

Hus was a Czech protestant who preached reform in Prague in the early fifteenth century. Like his English mentor, Wycliffe, he was condemned as a heretic and sent to the stake in 1415. This didn't have the desired effect on his followers, and his movement gained strength. Matters came to a head when in 1419 a Hussite band stormed the Town Hall, freed the Hussite prisoners there, and summarily dealt with resistance by throwing two Catholic councillors out of the window - an event magnificently labelled by history as the Defenestration of Prague. It isn't surprising that a bitter war ensued, lasting fifteen years until near stalemate enforced an uneasy truce.

The Town Hall is also site of the famous Astronomical Clock, a five hundred year old favourite of visitors to Prague. This mediaeval executive toy shows a calendar, represented by a complex assortment of dials looking like a squashed astrolabe; above it, a clock chimes the hour with a procession of moving figures. The story goes that its inventor was afterwards blinded, to prevent him from repeating the trick somewhere else. In revenge, he stopped the clock, which then took a hundred years to restart.

I'd now covered more than a mile, and by all accounts was well into Extra Time. But to give up without seeing Wenceslas Square was out of the question. So I compromised, finding my way to the near end, and sitting on a bollard while I mentally walked the length of it and back.

More a boulevard than a square, Václavské Náměstí stretches fully half a mile, between buildings varying in style from nineteenth century elegance to modern concrete and glass. At its far end the National Museum stands on a slight rise, overlooking the monument to St. Wenceslas and other Czech saints.

If Hradčany is the seat of power, and the Old Town Square that of commerce and tourism, then this is the political hub of Prague. Surrounded by the sophisticated hum of urban life, I could scarcely imagine the Soviet tanks crashing across this very spot after the so-called "Prague Spring" of 1968. It was here that student Jan Palach burned himself to death the following year in protest at the clampdown by Warsaw Pact troops; here, too, took place the demonstrations of 1989 which led to the resignation of the Communist government. And surely the most emotional moment of the Velvet Revolution in Prague was that when Alexander Dubček, displaced and disgraced leader of the doomed 1968 reform movement, stood on a balcony here and addressed the Praguers to a tumultuous reception.

It had been worth the extra walk. Reluctantly I dragged myself back to the present, and then to the Old Town Square again... where the Astronomical Clock was about to perform.

I watched from among a horde of tourists as the hour began to chime. The two doors at the top opened, and behind them marched a procession of figures: Christ and the Twelve Apostles. Below them gyrated the figures of Greed, Vanity, Death and Heresy, the latter two shown as a skeleton and a Turk. With the last Apostle, a cockerel appeared and flapped its wings in the doorway. And that was that for another hour.

Fully content, I at last turned wearily for the bus and home. And walked into a painful dilemma.

An organ recital was about to begin in St. Nicholas' Church; the programme listed outside included one of my favourite pieces. Temptation overwhelmed me.

But a small voice somewhere inside said a desperate no. It was now early evening; I had not been to bed all day, and had walked far farther than I could escape with impunity. Already I was in for big trouble in the next day or so. There was only one sensible decision, if I thought about it.

The problem was that, by reason of the long day, I had already been long on autopilot. When I tried to consult my brain for a rational opinion, it briefly woke up, mindlessly grunted a habitual "no surrender", rolled over and went back to sleep.

Under normal circumstances, I thought belligerently, there would have been no question. So I was damned if I would be deprived of a pleasure I would otherwise certainly have enjoyed. It would make the perfect end to the day. And yet...? Stalemate.

Fifteen minutes to decision time. I went into a cafe for another carbohydrate fix. It had the desired effect. I suddenly woke up long enough to realise that my bus went only to the zoo - which had closed two hours ago. If I didn't shift fast, I could be sleeping on a park bench.

Fortunately the bus was still running. My resentment collapsed as I reached my bed. An hour or two later I was on my way out of Prague, just far enough to find a nice, quiet patch of woodland where I could pull well off the road. And sleep the clock round.

CHAPTER V: FROM BOHEMIA'S WOODS AND FIELDS

> Rest I seek not, hope nor love,
>
> Nor a friend to know me,
>
> All I seek, the heaven above,
>
> And the road below me.

> (Robert Louis Stevenson: Songs of Travel)

I woke up - late - to a wonderful day of hazy sunshine, and looked out on an idyllic spot.

Last night I had pulled on to a forestry track for a hundred yards, anxious only to be away from the road and relatively invisible. Morning showed pine woods on three sides, while on the fourth a wide acreage of spring wheat soon disappeared into the mist. True, there was an enormous muck-heap a dozen yards off, but who was I at this stage to be complaining about smells?

I was already very tired from the previous day, and could expect to become much more so as the full effects caught up. It was pointless to hurry, and anyway for once I felt tolerant of idleness. So I idled until mid-day, passing the time pleasantly in drinking tea, reading, drinking more tea and watching the woods go about their daily business.

A pheasant was fascinated by the van. He strutted up and down past it like a sentry, waving his tail and screeching. A red squirrel was swinging like a miniature Tarzan through the trees a few yards away, followed by a very tame jay. Somewhere behind a strange bird called, with the bell-like clarity of a nightingale but deeper and more resonant.

At last I set off, feeling rather more human. It was all cross-country to Pardubice, and the drive more enjoyable than any so far. This part of Bohemia has great tracts of forest, some certainly managed but much looking as if nothing had changed since the evolution of trees. The intervening fields were neatly harrowed ready for the drill, and here and there whole families worked together planting potatoes.

For the first time I saw a couple of horse teams. The soil they turned was light and sandy and looked very dry, as if it hadn't rained here for days. It wasn't going to today, either; the weather remained glorious, and my skin hummed with the effects of yesterday's sun.

To the West, the provincial town of Pardubice is infamous for manufacturing the plastic explosive, Semtex. Among the racing fraternity, though, it has a ring like that of Aintree; for it gives its name to the annual Grand Pardubice Steeplechase, the Czech Republic's Grand National. This is more of a cross-country race than a steeplechase as the English would understand it. Its variety of fences includes walls, banks, streams and the infamous Taxis fence, an oxer and ditch reputed to make Becher's Brook look like something out of a Pony Club gymkhana. I wanted to see for myself. And if there was training or even racing in progress, so much the better.

Certainly this was horse country. I passed a couple of stables, each with a field of rather tatty jumps and a number of horses, oozing boredom in their small individual earth paddocks.

Pardubice was suddenly ahead, and I had given absolutely no thought as to how I would find the course. But I was lucky, as my relatively minor road directly passed it.

The entrance, round the back behind the stands, was fiercely guarded by a determined looking gatekeeper, who grumpily told me I couldn't come in. I chatted him up a bit, and he began to soften; then, producing photographs, told him all about my own horse Tim, and he began to purr. Obviously a bloke with the right priorities. But the gate stayed closed. With sudden inspiration, I told him of a friend who planned to enter his own horse in the Grand Pardubice. In fact the plans were two years old, and had foundered when the chaser got a "leg", but he wasn't to know that. Improvising rapidly as I sensed him begin to crack, I added that my friend had asked me to do some homework for him, and particularly to check out the size of the Taxis fence.

That pressed the right button. With the ghoulish pleasure of a morgue attendant taking someone to view the corpse, he took out his keys, with a "mum's the word" gesture. As he was about to take me on to the course, somebody called him. I escaped, to wander at will around the near fences, before he rapidly gave chase and frog-marched me off to where I was supposed to be going.

This was some of the best ground for galloping horses on that I'd ever seen, sandy underfoot yet springy with old turf. Fresh prints spoke of daily use, but training was over for the day - just as well, as otherwise I would never have been allowed near the track.

The course itself was beautifully laid out, with wide, well-built fences, an attractive stand of woodland and freshly painted white rails - a far cry from our uniform, functional tracks. I dreamed of Tim, a few years off the clock and an afternoon's fun; but changed my mind when I saw the Taxis.

On the approach, it looked scruffy and disappointing. It was just a hedge, I thought with contempt, not particularly big and with great gaps. But the sting was on the far side. The ditch was wicked; seven feet deep, with a trickle of water and an innocent yellow splash of celandines. The width was colossal - thoroughly dangerous, and with a sharp, steep lip to the edge that could break a horse down if it landed short.

Any aspirations to the Grand Pardubice, I decided, were indefinitely shelved.

Getting more and more friendly, my new chum now took me on a tour of the stands. He showed me the list of winners which included Chris Collins and Stephen's Society, who took the trophy home to Britain in 1977. At last, as I was gratefully saying goodbye, he found me a copy of the programme from the previous year's race, and I raised my street cred by pointing out Quirinus, the winner. Poor Quirinus; his triumph earned him a trip to Aintree the following spring, only to go to post in vain for the Grand National that never was. For the race failed to start properly, and was declared void.

Quirinus was in good company. Also in the racecard was an advert to draw potential National spectators, with an all-in trip at six thousand krowns - about three hundred pounds, a fortune for the average Czech. Steeplechasing knows too many ways to break your heart.

*

In search of lunch and the odd signpost, I made for the town centre. Pardubice, I soon discovered, was a dump; a small provincial town that had grown rapidly - and without taste - through its industry. Why bother, I wondered sourly, to go to all the trouble of exporting their Semtex via Libya to Ireland, when I could see a much better use for it here?

Only Saturday lunchtime, and everything was shut; except for a rather sleazy cafe, where the town's bored and aimless youth went for its weekend thrills. An equally bored and aimless waitress brought me tea that turned out to be vile coffee, and I rapidly rethought lunch in favour of something out of the tin-box back at HQ.

A few miles out of town I stopped for a huge meal, fending off a freak swarm of ladybirds; then dragged my bed out into the open for a long, lazy afternoon in the sun.

*

The evening stint, entirely on minor roads and lanes, was unforgettable.

I left the main road at Chrudim. Its puce-coloured Town Hall couldn't be passed without a closer look. I stretched my legs in the square, then sat on the edge of a monument like a petrified fountain and admired another Gothic, twin-towered church. Behind was a quiet little park with a statue to Jan Hus.

Then on into the countryside, here still flat and open like much of the Czech Republic so far, but with a hint of promise in the glimpse of higher ground and more forest ahead to the south. Immediately outside Prague, winter had come firmly back into control. The beech, birch and occasional oak dotted among the pines were all quite bare, the chestnut sticky buds only just beginning unwillingly to swell and crack. When I reached the uplands and began to climb, there was snow still lying in gullies and against north-facing banks. Evidently this part of the world experiences long, hard winters.

And now I came out of the denser forests into some of the loveliest country imaginable. Among rolling hills fringed with woodland were alpine-style villages, whose neat, clean lines were worlds away from the rough edges and dangling wires of the north-west. The houses were mostly chalets, their red-tiled roofs steeply sloping and often asymmetric; outside each was an enormous pile of logs. Who, I wondered, had done all that hewing of wood, and did they have a chain saw? The van began to smell sweetly of woodsmoke.

Again, the land was ploughed and ready for seed, but as yet nothing grew; while the huge steaming middens suggested many animals, with not a grazing beast to be seen. The pasture wore that peculiar flat, grey look of very recent thaw, so presumably all the stock was still in winter quarters indoors. In a few weeks' time, I guessed, the valleys would be alive to the sound of cowbells.

It wasn't only the villages that charmed. There was a simplicity, almost an unreality, about the rounded contours of the landscape, improbably pleasing to the eye, and heightened by a lack of the usual twentieth century impedimenta. The few houses in open country were square and uncomplicated, like a child's drawing, and occasionally a solitary church or round stone tower stood out on a hilltop. The effect was strangely mediaeval, as if it were a landscape glimpsed through the window of a Renaissance portrait, or a backcloth for Olivier's Henry V.

Towards' dusk the woods thickened again, with ranks of gloomy pines to darken the steep-sided valleys. I was fussy in my choice of a campsite, and twice nearly bogged the van in forestry tracks before settling for the corner of a field. Once again I had finished in the dark.

The delight of the afternoon was fading. It worried me that I couldn't seem to get my timing right. Day after day I was late to bed, getting up and starting late the next morning and so perpetuating the whole cycle, the constant need to catch up on myself.

No sooner had I stopped than a car drew up and two men got out. Nervously I locked myself inside and opened the window a crack to them. But they turned out to be only a couple of curious young policemen. After a glance at my passport and a few pleasantries, they politely wished me good night and went peaceably on their way.

*

I was late the next morning too, but that was the least of my problems.

The long day in Prague had caught up. I felt worse than I had for nearly a year. My chest throbbed badly, the slightest movement increasing the pressure, while a steam hammer thumped inside my head and black spots swam around like tadpoles in my optical fluids.

My feelings were a blend of profound depression and utter panic; scarcely a week into the trip, and already things were falling apart. The fear got worse when I tried to go for a pee. I couldn't even make the few yards to the shelter of the trees.

There was nothing for it but lie still and wait to recharge. At least this gave ample time to think things through, to identify what was going wrong and, more importantly, decide what to do about it.

For a start, the hectic pre-departure week was taking its toll. If I'd had a chance to build up some reserves before leaving, there would have been rather more in hand to offset the binges of those long walks in Berlin and Prague. But reserves or not, I must obviously live more economically, and settle for a more superficial view.

And there were many other problems and mistakes. I hadn't allowed extra time for traffic, finding campsites, or just for getting lost on country roads. Moreover, washing self, clothes and utensils, and also cooking, were harder than usual, although the simplicity of my menus more than made up for the last.

Worse, the more exhausted I had become, the harder it was to make concessions or to rethink my plans. My tired brain just locked into a rut, or shut down altogether, as it had over the Prague concert, leaving me to go stumbling blindly on through my pre-determined routine and unable to judge whether it was too much.

Finally, I hadn't managed a decent wash for two days, nor even cleared up the cocoa I'd spilt yesterday; every bowl and pan was dirty, the fuse had blown on the kettle and I was already on the spare gas canister.

Even then I didn't doubt that, somehow, the journey would be completed. But at present it promised to happen only mechanically, in a haze of exhaustion and double vision; not the Great Adventure I had envisioned, symbol of ultimate control over The Beast, but a hideous grudging chore in which It would have the last laugh at my puny attempts to dominate It.

I rested for some hours, and gradually some strength seeped back. With it my spirits began to climb to their knees. Slowly, as the problems came forward and identified themselves, a few partial solutions came to mind. Hardest of all would be accepting the need to prune the programme a bit. On the other hand, taking stock, I could find positive entries on the balance sheet. For example, although yesterday's conversation with the gateman at Pardubice had been my longest for a week, I wasn't troubled by loneliness.

When I had first proposed the trip, one of the commonest reactions among my friends was: "But surely you're not going alone?" It was hard to explain that it was better so; that the physical demands of being in company constituted a luxury well beyond my budget.

Imagine that you are slightly drunk, taking tea with your mother-in-law and the Bishop, and trying desperately to appear sober. The level of effort involved is about the same as that which the average ME person makes in company. None of us wishes to be, nor yet to appear to other people as, constantly slow, unresponsive or plain dim. The animation you need to raise your game, even just a little, in front of others is supplied by nervous energy or adrenaline, which does a good temporary job but burns you out in no time.

By contrast, the hours of driving, although sometimes overlong, were neither stressful nor physical. Of course, you need to be alert; but it's a passive alertness, without the need to interact with another person: someone observing you, perhaps assessingly, perhaps even - if a stranger to ME - rather baffled by your inadequacies.

Loneliness isn't a matter of geography. For me, it will always be identified with the inability to tolerate company for long; with a situation where you might pass a week, or even two, without speaking to anyone face to face; except perhaps for a couple of words with the postman. Not because I lacked friends ready to pop round for coffee and a chat - indeed, if I hadn't been singularly fortunate in my friends, the last few years would have been incomparably bleak - but because the necessary energy was already earmarked two or three times over for something more imperative to my existence.

To be alone within the same unchanging set of walls in a static world is one thing; whereas to be alone whizzing along in a tin box, with new horizons speeding towards you and fascinating worlds unravelling beneath your wheels, is entirely another matter; something from a different planet.

*

Finally, around early afternoon, I made it into the driving seat and trundled down the road to Pernštejn Castle. Although the castle itself had been the original reason to come here, I must admit that the hope of a restaurant and a decent lunch was rather more attractive.

Yes, it did have a restaurant, but it was full just now. Meanwhile, Pernštejn Castle was after all rather special.

It was the ultimate Gothic castle. A Disney-like jumble of towers and turrets, each looking as if it had been built on to the last as an afterthought, it perched on a crag, peering malevolently down through thick, damp forests at the village of the same name below. It might have been the model for Gormenghast.

It deserved at least a closer look. I ambled slowly past the two fierce-looking gatehouses and over the dry moat, and before I realised it was standing by the till. To turn back now would have looked deliberately mean. I was committed. So much for cancelling the active part of the day.

Unfortunately, Pernštejn wasn't designed for conserving energy. The architect had preferred vertical to lateral thinking, and the sum of all the staircases vastly exceeded that of the corridors in length. The guided tour was compulsory. I spent most of the upward half of it straggling far behind, to the gentle concern of the student guide, and my own embarrassment. Fortunately the commentary was in Czech, so the fact that I missed most of it was irrelevant.

It was worth the effort. From the top, the view was amazing. The jungle of rooftops made the castle seem even more complex than from below. Kestrels squabbled among the tiles, swerving confidently under bridges and arches to dive-bomb each other, screaming loudly.

The interior was dull - at least to start with. But for the occasional wooden chair and a chest big enough to hide at least three bodies in, the early rooms were mostly empty and definitely un-spooky. I soon stopped looking for Steerpike or Prunesquallor round every corner. The guide had kept the best rooms till last: a picture gallery, with seventeenth century family portraits, and a series from the life of Elijah; an armoury bristling with vicious-looking pikes and a rack of flintlock rifles; and an extraordinary room with elaborate cornices and panelling painted very convincingly on to a perfectly plane wall, with similar "oil paintings" and "frames". This last room was disconcerting, almost surreal. It was a relief to emerge into fresh air and three dimensions.

The restaurant came up to expectations. A charming head waiter patiently explained the menu, and although I still wasn't entirely sure what I ate, it was a gourmet meal compared to the alternative. Afterwards, I took a good four hours to sleep it off, without moving any further than the car park.

*

North of Brno, at which I was ultimately if circuitously aiming, lie the limestone hills and valleys of the Moravsky Kras. This is typical karst country, where deep ravines score the hillsides, and rivers disappear frothing down sinkholes to pop up tamely half a mile away, dissolving intricate cave systems from the rock over the millennia.

It is the caves that are the attraction here. Like Cheddar, the area is packed in summer with tourists who come to visit its four show caves. The best of these, Punkevní Jeskyne, offers underground boat rides as part of the trip.

The Punkevní was well hidden. The roads hereabouts necessarily follow the ravines, making for a convoluted web in which you lose all sense of direction. My map gave up without a fight, replacing the web with a few straight lines drawn apparently at random. It led me to Sloup, too far north, without so much as a glimpse of a sinkhole. True, there was a cave here, but it wasn't the one I wanted and anyway it didn't open until June.

There was also a small supermarket, and this was much better news. I was out of bread, and here they sold crusty rolls of a kind not tasted since the invention of the sliced loaf. Hungry again, I sank two straight off without even stopping for butter, and forgave myself completely for getting lost.

For getting lost the first time, anyway. Half an hour later I rolled back northwards into Sloup, convinced at the time that I was heading due south. It was third time lucky when I finally hit a spectacular limestone gorge. Where it widened briefly into a grassy stretch by the river, I found the perfect place to camp. And, for once, in good time.

*

The day began on a relaxed and optimistic note. One of unusual luxury, too; for I'd made good use of my leisure the evening before.

It was bliss to eat breakfast off sparklingly clean plates; even more so to drink my tea without first filtering out the bits of porridge between my teeth. Not, you understand, that I'm normally in any way sloppy over domestic chores. Perish the thought. But after years of such choices as that between either wearing clean clothes or eating a hot meal on a given day, you quickly learn that re-using an unwashed pan doesn't necessarily mean a horrible death from food poisoning.

The meadow by which I'd slept was thick with flowers: a white feathery sedum like orpine, the naked daisies of coltsfoot, and blue anemones like those which had bloomed in my garden two months ago. Spring was later than ever here; in a strange climatic inversion the sunlit uplands were well ahead of the murky ravine floor. A pair of squirrels scampering ahead of me along the road were still in winter woollies. Obviously "red" - small bodies, huge tails and tufty ears - they were actually a sort of dirty brown.

Down from the meadow the gorge closed in once more, becoming deeper and more imposing, and forcing the road to burrow under a great overhang. The river came and went, now flowing fast and broad in the open, now diving into a sinkhole or bursting from the mouth of a cave.

Finally the rock drew back under sheer two hundred foot cliffs, and there was the Punkevní Cave.

*

Limestone cave systems, such as these in Moravia, are formed by the action of water on rock over thousands of years. Acid rain, in fact; not the vile sulphurous sludge which has wiped out great tracts of European forest in our own times, but weak carbonic acid formed by the dissolving of atmospheric carbon dioxide.

The chemical reactions following its seepage into natural fissures can eventually turn cracks into chasms, air pockets into cathedral-like caverns, a slow drip into a thunderous underground cataract. In the reverse process, water running down a cave wall or dripping from a roof leaves limestone deposits which may grow, grain by grain, into wonderful or weird formations: the linen-drape effect of limestone curtain, or the knobs of cauliflower stone, the familiar stalactites and stalagmites or, where a through draught takes a hand, fantastic sideways-curling helictites.

It is these formations which make for the fascination of cave-systems; these and the rival fascination of discovering whole new worlds underground, fathoms beneath the familiar one above.

The Punkevní Cave and its relations run for miles, through twisting, plunging and climbing passages, many of which are broad and high enough to walk comfortably. With the help of wooden walkways and steps where necessary, and the luxury of electric lighting throughout, some of the largest chambers and the most striking formations have been made accessible to the ordinary surface-dweller.

Not so the waterways; the boats weren't running this early in the year. Again the guided tour was unavoidable, and I passed through the heavy door into the damp and dripping underworld in the wake of a large coach party. Inside, the limestone formations began almost at once. Spectacular formations: whole caverns of pillars and curtains in colours ranging from palest cream through ochre to sepia, smooth as mother-of-pearl to the touch; rows of tiny needle-like stalactites clinging to the ceilings, each following the line of an infinitesimal crack.

There was much upping and downing, and I lagged increasingly far behind. This was an advantage, as solitude gave more atmosphere and better views. But when the guide began switching off lights behind, as she thought, the last client, I began to find myself always straining towards the half-light round the next corner. At one long stair section I was left in pitch darkness, and had to set off my camera flash to see around me. At last the way began to slope downhill again. I was gaining steadily when the yellow electric light gave way to a rather grey daylight, and I caught up the party at the foot of the Macocha Abyss.

To describe it as a pothole would be accurate but miserably inadequate. Nearly five hundred feet deep and probably a hundred yards across, it made Alum Pot look like a rabbit hole. The walls were vertical, except for the great domed cavern at the end where we stood. A handful of twigs at the top moved, and turned into tiny human figures looking down at us from a precarious edge.

Whole trees had fallen in, lying like matchsticks among rocks covered in moss and fern above a bank of old, dirty snow. At the bottom, a few feet beneath the rail over which we leaned, was an evil, slimy green lake, draining in a thin stream deep into the cave system. "...Where Alph, the sacred river, ran, Through caverns measureless to man, Down to a sunless sea..." The whole was a place of indescribable desolation, a twilight, malevolent spot whose coldness wasn't entirely a matter of temperature: the abode of trolls, or other nameless horrors.

The group was very quiet as we set off for home; then shook itself defiantly and began to sing, in Czech, "Hi-ho! Hi-ho! It's off to work we go!" This time I kept them in sight, and at the exit just managed to avoid being locked underground for the night by the diligent guide.

But the spell of the underworld, or maybe the disorientation of its corkscrew passages, was still heavy on me. For when I tried later to escape from the Moravsky Kras, I headed firmly south for Brno, yet found myself once again... at Sloup.

CHAPTER VI: DOWN AMONG THE DEAD MEN

Convivial friends have all gone,

Death has trampled them down one after another;

We were in one wine-bout at life's party,

They got drunk a round or so ahead of us.

(Omar Khayyam: Ruba'iyaat)

Slavkov is a tiny village east of Brno, barely distinguished by its château. Students of military history, not to mention readers of Tolstoy, would better recognise it under its Austrian name: Austerlitz.

Here, as described in "War and Peace", Napoleon routed a joint Russian-Austrian army, complete with its two Emperors and under the overall command of the Russian General Kutuzov. The so-called "Battle of the Three Emperors" was fought out over most of the land between Slavkov and Brno. Today it is commemorated by the Mohyla Miru, or Monument to Peace, which stands along with a museum on Pratzen Hill at the centre of the battlefield.

This was some distance from Slavkov itself. I stopped several times to ask the way, finding in the process more almost perfect parallels between Czech and Russian. I knew I was getting warm when wayside crosses began to appear along the road and in the surrounding farmland. Soon a succession of signposts fielded me neatly, directed me along a series of twists and turns, and dropped me at the spot.

Just in time; it was almost dark. From the top of the hill I could see the lights of Brno, seeming to stretch for miles. All around, thrushes were singing an ecstatic goodnight. Within fifteen minutes they were all in bed, and the only noise came from the angry pheasants which I disturbed as I looked for a loo.

Tonight I was fed, watered and horizontal by nine - much better. On each of the last two days I had been out of bed for just five hours, and the long rests were building up some reserves again. Even my face looked better, I convinced myself as I squinted in the driving mirror; one or two of the extra wrinkly bits made by the first week were smoothing out.

It was an eerie place to sleep. All around, less than two centuries ago, 27,000 men had died violently. But I slept like the dead - if more briefly - and no ghostly clash of arms disturbed my dreams.

*

The monument wasn't very inspiring by daylight; just a concave-sided concrete pyramid topped with a spire. But the museum was well worth the visit.

It was high on pictures and low on exhibits, though there were a few cases of very serious-looking sabres and lots of bits and stirrups dug up on the battlefield over the years. The best display by far was a layout of toy soldiers, with a detailed relief map showing the dispositions of the two sides.

To my ignorance, Kutuzov's position appeared the better. His battle lines were neatly drawn up on the high ground of Pratzen Hill, while the French seemed rather haphazardly deployed below, with the disadvantage of the lower ground. But this impression, of course, was part of the plan. Luring the Austro-Russian forces off the hill to the south, Napoleon smashed into his enemy's rear with one of his characteristic flanking actions, cryptically referred to by historians as "manoeuvres sur les derrières". By mid-day, he was himself in possession of Pratzen, and Kutuzov was in retreat.

Perhaps Kutuzov's heavy drinking bout on the eve of battle had blurred his judgement. That, or other distractions - he travelled with three girls in his baggage train, and was reputed to require the attentions of all three on a single night. Although already turned sixty, he was by no means finished by the crushing defeat, and was later to have the last laugh on Napoleon.

*

The road into Brno was an avenue of tall, beautiful trees. They were familiar yet strange; it was a few minutes before I recognised them as elms, having not seen one over ten feet high since the ravages in Britain of Dutch Elm Disease twenty-odd years ago.

The town wasn't so beautiful. It was busy, noisy and rather dingy, with the sort of faded elegance you might associate with a Middle Eastern capital. The streets fairly rattled with trams, racing here and there like dodgem cars. It made for stimulating driving.

I parked near the station and walked along cobbled streets to the smaller of the two town squares. It held a busy fruit market, and I sat on the vantage point of its central fountain, enjoying everyone else's buzzing activity and my own idleness.

From one of the irregular angles of the square, a narrow street led up to the cathedral. It was clearly visible by the needle-sharp twin spires - and not by much else, for it was closely hemmed in by tall buildings. Inside, the tallness of the nave gave back a sense of space, drawing the gaze down to the further end where three slender stained glass windows stretched from floor to ceiling. Down each side, enclosed by walls of plaster where the eye searched for stone, were four arched chapels.

On the far side, the ground fell away almost vertically past the remains of citadel walls, now shored up by timber. Below, partly screened by the thin new leaves of a lime tree that clung precariously to the edge, the traffic roared by. On a clear day you can see, it is said, to Vienna.

I needed two things urgently. Back in the slightly claustrophobic streets, I found them: a spare gas cylinder, and lunch. Goulash and dumplings are staple Czech fare; comments in the guide books range from the patronising to the scathing, but to me they tasted wonderful after ten days' living mostly out of tins and packets.

It was as well I had left my final visit until afterwards, as it would have been seriously damaging to the most robust appetite.

The Capuchin church is a bland building of apricot-coloured plaster overlooking half-a-dozen dark stone figures of various divines. The church itself, glimpsed through the locked grille, looked unremarkable. You would have passed it without a second glance - if it weren't for the crypt.

A couple of centuries ago, it was common for anyone who was - or had been - anybody, to be interred in open coffins among the ex-monks in the crypt of the Capuchins. Whether the site was believed to confer extra sanctity on the departed, or whether it was just a fashionable idea which caught on, no-one now can remember. Quite simply, it became *de rigueur* for the smart set to join the party. No self-respecting corpse would be seen dead anywhere else.

And there they still lie, mummified in the fusty underground air, lined up to be admired, as they were in life, by the hoi polloi. Their faces are still disconcertingly human, although the cheekbones protrude and the lips are drawn back over yellow teeth; their once fine clothing is faded to a monochrome sepia. A sign over the entry reads MEMENTO MORI; in case the message hasn't got home, another inside reminds you with grisly relish, "TU" FUI; "EGO" ERIS. I was once you; you will become me.

Whoever drew up the placings had a macabre sense of humour. Immediately inside the door was an alcove with three members of the same family. A tablet over their coffins named them: the brothers Grimm.

*

Gears crashing, I ducked and dodged among the trams with fierce concentration. " 'Ego' eris?" Not just yet, if I could help it.

I was trying to get to the fruit market to stock up, but the one-way system defeated me. After a three-point turn in a pedestrian precinct I bottled out and went to a boring but friendly supermarket. A few minutes later I was on the first motorway for days, and heading south-west for the Slovak border.

It was only four months since Czechoslovakia had followed up the "Velvet Revolution" with the so-called "Velvet Divorce", splitting into two separate countries. Would the Slovaks, I wondered, stand on their dignity, making a point of border formalities?

Not a bit of it. They were so laid-back as almost to be apologetic for the fuss. At the Czech end, there was barely time to show my passport; while the charming young Slovak officer obviously wanted to ask questions, but was prevented by the language barrier. What he really meant was, "Anything to declare?" but what he actually managed was to point to the back and say, "Televisor...?" I smiled broadly and said, "No, no televisor!" At which he smiled equally broadly and waved me through.

Beyond, the landscape gradually changed to a sort of sweeping downland with echoes of east Bohemia, but more intimate. Neat orchards and vineyards covered the south-facing hillsides, and a splash of early blossom caught my eye. The spring advanced visibly as I drove south, with the roadside willows and birches taking on a green flush. By the time Bratislava appeared on the horizon, the grass verges were taking on that pregnant look that precedes violent growth.

Intending to enter the new Slovak capital by the minor road that runs along the Danube through Devin, I left the motorway at Stupava. Not a moment too soon; could those hideous skyscrapers ahead really be part of my destination? At least the turgid, swampy river by the road was not the real thing, but only, I discovered to my infinite relief, a tributary of the main river.

I came round a bend to find myself simultaneously at Devin, and the Danube. It was perfect timing. The sun was setting behind me so that Devin's ruined castle, and the river, were drenched in amber light.

Jumping on the brakes, I stopped under the castle mound by a sign that almost certainly said "No Parking" in Slovak, and began to plod slowly up the bank for a better view.

And received a wonderful and wholly unexpected surprise. The two restful days produced a dividend; for instead of taking me up a couple of dozen feet then going on strike, my legs kept working, taking me up and up, with only a few brief rests, all the way to the top.

I nearly fell over a courting couple; but by now I was grinning like a Cheshire cat with a delight that must have been infectious, for the girl only grinned back and turned again to her lover. I removed myself to a decent distance and stood hard under the castle walls, savouring a wonderful moment: the elation of the achievement, the glowing light against the castle walls, and Europe's most charismatic river flowing darkly red as the sun plunged seemingly into its waters.

At this hour Devin Castle was closed to the public, but I couldn't stop now. High as a kite, I climbed on to the parapet and walked right round, not caring who saw me; then sat on what remained of the keep, watching until the sunset had faded to an afterglow.

Me too; time for bed. I made my way slowly down again to the van, to find Trouble looming over it in military uniform.

The sign did indeed say No Parking, and I grovelled abjectly. Fortunately the two young military policemen were extremely nice, pointing at the sign in a finger-wagging way, and backing up the gesture with a halting, "Nicht hier stehen!" With more tact than I'd deserved, they didn't even wait to see me off.

I wondered if they would have been so tolerant if they'd seen me cavorting on the castle walls half an hour before.

*

Taking my cue from the guide books, and also from the unattractive Brno, I was fully prepared to dislike Bratislava. But I couldn't help being cheered on the road in by the bright red lamp-posts against the pale green of the new leaves. True, the high rise buildings at the end of the road were also pale green, but they were far enough off to ignore.

Much new road-building was in progress. I wondered where the money was coming from for such extravagance, for Slovakia is supposed to be financially the worse for the split from the Czech Republic. Certainly the severance, instigated mainly by the government in Bratislava, didn't please everyone. There are many who think that, had a referendum been held, Czechoslovakia might have remained intact. Others disagree: whereas the Czechs, they argued, are mostly influenced by Austria and the West, Slovakia on the other hand, with a history of nearly a millennium under Hungarian rule, looks eastward; the opposing orientation of the two parts would make the whole unviable, once the unifying blanket of Communism was folded away.

If this is a major reason for secession, however, then Slovakia's attitude towards its 600,000 ethnic Hungarians - a significant number in a total population of 5,000,000 - is surprising. Hungarian, effectively the second language in Slovakia, has been actively suppressed. Bilingual road signs, once frequent, have been banned, broadcasting in Hungarian restricted. Is this just a temporary result of self-consciousness, a sense of the fragility of Slovakia's new identity? Perhaps, when the state is more solidly established, a new self-confidence will allow the return of the old live-and-let-live.

Bratislava itself lacks harmony in its mix of old and new. Brash development features somewhere in most big cities, especially those of the eastern bloc, but is especially obtrusive here. Large areas have been bulldozed to make way for new building, and a major road now cuts ruthlessly through the centre of the Old Town, leaving the citadel and the cathedral facing each other across a hundred yards of naked concrete, an estranged couple.

The citadel, walled in with dull brick, hadn't much to recommend it. Even the trams avoided it, burrowing underneath instead through a long tunnel, and it was a long weary trudge to the top. In the thirties, the dingy houses here were an infamous haunt of prostitutes; today the street was deserted.

The square turreted castle at the top houses a museum, with gardens laid out pleasantly as a park. From the promenade along their walls is a tremendous view over city and river. Just a few hundred yards away is the new suspension bridge, the elliptical top of its single pillar levitating like a space-ship over a forest of wires.

I left by the south gatehouse and took the steep street to the cathedral, dicing with death on the main road. But it was closed; I had a brief glimpse of a tall nave and three high windows as at Brno, before I was shooed out again.

Back along the city walls to the van, deafened by the traffic. There wasn't much to keep me here; a quick run into the centre to change money, and it would be time to get out.

The cash was more hassle than it was worth. After the usual wrestle with the one-way system and parking, I was directed up two flights of stairs to the Exchange desk. A Rosa Klebb lookalike sat with her back to the counter, chatting to a friend and generally indicating that customers were an unnecessary interruption to her social life; and that if they didn't speak Slovak, they were in no position to disagree.

Having that morning decided that I liked Bratislava, I stormed out in a fury and couldn't wait to leave. Another bank, another failure; but at the third attempt I received both Slovak currency and generous Slovak courtesy, and simmered down.

I called at the post office, and found an enormous echoing vault with tiles and glass roof like a Victorian swimming pool; looked for the tourist office on

Leningradská Street, only to find that Leningradská (now politically incorrect) had changed its name and the office - at the far end, of course - was now a building site; called in at a bookshop where the astonishingly low prices quickly tempted me to buy too many books; and decided that Bratislava was exhausted, and it was time for even the most enthusiastic tourist to leave.

*

South east of Bratislava is Slovakia's most controversial construction project, the Gabčíkovo Dam.

The project was conceived in 1978, as a joint Czechoslovak-Hungarian venture, with Austrian backing. The idea of diverting the Danube into an enormous canal, feeding dams at Gabčíkovo in Slovakia, and Nagymaros in Hungary, seemed a good one. It promised to provide enough hydro-electric power to replace many out-of-date and inefficient power stations. But massive environmentalist opposition persuaded the Hungarians and Austrians to pull out, leaving the Slovaks stubbornly pushing ahead on their own.

There are convincing arguments on both sides. Supporters claim that Slovakia's energy capacity will be doubled, by electricity cleanly produced as opposed to that supplied by burning the heavily-polluting brown coal; and that in the process it will become possible to control the otherwise frequent flooding of one of the country's richest agricultural regions.

The opposition point out that this very agriculture is being damaged by over-drying of the soil, only one of many environmental objections. Meanwhile, the new canal has cut off a number of villages beside the river; villages that now lie squeezed between it and the border, whose occupants face long journeys to visit relatives and neighbours formerly only half a mile away.

Among the wrangling, the Slovak government has grimly pursued its course; after all, no argument is so convincing as a fait accompli. Now the moment of truth has arrived when the dam at Gabčíkovo is ready to begin operating. One way or another, the whole pudding is about to be proved.

Thirty miles out of Bratislava, something foreign appeared in the landscape to the south, something that didn't quite belong. A few more miles, and this materialised into a long dyke running parallel to the road: the line of the canal.

Pulling off the main road, I passed through a village then brazenly took a contractors' service road on to the dyke for a closer look. The canal was enormous, almost as wide as the course of the Danube at Bratislava. But whereas there the water had been moving very fast, here it didn't seem to be flowing at all. The only movement was a restless sloshing from side to side; a caged liquid beast.

Gabčíkovo village, some miles further on, was demurely attractive with its avenue of flowering almond trees leading straight to the ochre and white church in the centre. It looked altogether too staid and respectable a place to lend its name to a monster that had raised so much spleen.

The monster itself was a mile out of town. Near some brand-new apartment blocks, home to the construction workers, was an embryonic but already mushrooming industrial estate. The road swept on and up, right over the dam. There was space on the top to park and take a proper look at the two enormous locks. A couple of gigantic barges hid almost invisibly at the bottom of one, dwarfed by the scale.

Whatever the pros and cons of the Gabčíkovo Dam, I couldn't help being impressed by the sheer size of the structure, the optimism of the venture. To divert Europe's second largest river, and thus to harness its entire power, were ideas that were incomprehensible, almost laughable in their audacity. Yet they had been realised; their substance was before my eyes.

The villages around were as pretty as Gabčíkovo, and as full of blossom; for I had come a long way south in two days, and this area has the warmest climate of all Slovakia. I was tempted to idle, and stop somewhere here overnight. But the tyrannical schedule demanded that I should be well into Hungary already, and I was uncomfortably aware of the difficulties of making up time if I got behind. So instead of continuing to the border at Komárno, I made directly for the nearest crossing at Medvedov. This would put me directly on the Györ-Budapest motorway. Before very long I would be wishing I had done anything but.

I lingered on the bridge across the Danube - now back on its own course - then crossed into Hungary in record speed, sparing a thought for the endless line of lorries queueing on the opposite side.

Two things about Hungary hit me at once. The first, that it was somehow cleaner than much of the Czech Republic and Slovakia. The second, that Hungarian motorists drove like Jehu. The latter thought was prophetic.

*

The dog was lying in the centre lane. It was so big that at first I thought it was a deer.

I pulled on to the hard shoulder alongside, and went to look. It hard evidently only just been hit; it was still alive, and conscious, but its hind legs were useless, the back obviously broken. Although it was desperately thin, it was far too big for me to move myself.

I yanked out the warning triangle and put it a hundred yards back beside the outside lane. The dog yelped in pain as another car struck it, and I was almost running as I went to the lay-by for help.

A German motorist came to help, and managed to pull the dog to the hard shoulder. Duty done, he drove on, and I was left wondering how I could find a vet to put it down.

There was an emergency telephone at the lay-by, but the woman at the other end spoke only Hungarian. As I replaced the receiver a car pulled up, and I breathed a sigh of relief: the police.

There were two of them. The woman spoke German, but became silent as soon as it was obvious that I hadn't broken down. They were only paid to deal with problems on wheels.

I went to the other window, and pleaded with her colleague to help. He signed that he didn't understand, but reluctantly came to see what was the matter. I got the message across that the dog was seriously injured, and needed a vet. He didn't seem to understand what a vet was, but gestured to the gun at his belt. God help me, but I agreed with him; the animal couldn't be left to die slowly.

What followed was like a nightmare. I watched in horror and disbelief as, instead of approaching and shooting it cleanly, he stood where he was and randomly emptied a magazine into its body, yet without killing it. I alternately begged and shouted at him, showed him by pantomime what he should do, implored him to give me the gun and let me do it.

It was no good. Miraculously discovering his German, he rounded on me angrily and shouted that he wouldn't fire any more in a public place, that the bullets could riccochet off the concrete and hurt someone. The way he was spraying them around, he had a point.

As they drove off, the dog was still breathing, in shallow gasps. There was no one else around to ask for help. I jumped in the van and set off to try again to find a vet.

At a petrol station just off the motorway, I found an attendant who spoke German, and told him the story. He knew of no vet; the idea seemed strange to him. I suggested the telephone directory, but Hungary has not heard of Yellow Pages. What about the police? But he saw nothing unusual in the attitude I had found already, and thought I would be no luckier next time round. How I longed for a friendly British bobby, or even the gentle Slovak police.

In the end, I had to accept that there was absolutely nothing I could do. By now, an hour had passed, and I hoped fervently that nature - or the lack of it -

had taken its course. I simply got back in the van and drove on, feeling like the Priest and the Levite rolled into one, and utterly, utterly loathing myself for my inadequacy.

It was late, and dark, but I carried on as if pursued until I reached Budapest; then stopped uncaring by the main road, and lay awake all night.

The euphoria of the previous evening was barely a memory. I hated Hungary with all my heart, and wished to God I had never left home.

CHAPTER VII: BUDAPEST

Steep, descending layers, plumed all the way down
with trees... a sweep of the Danube, crossed by half-
a-dozen bridges... mediaeval pinnacles touched with
gilding and adorned by crockets... architectural dash
could scarcely go further.

(Patrick Leigh Fermor: Between the Woods and the Water)

At the campsite I hadn't reached the previous night, I got down to an
enormous batch of washing. Into the bowl went every stitch I'd had on the
previous day; an instinctive gesture of ritual cleansing.

A piece of baling twine between two trees made a passable washing line,
even if it was groaning under the weight. I wondered what inlookers to the van
would make of the line of knickers hanging from the curtain wire.

I wasn't prepared to like Budapest very much, the Hungarians still less so.
But both tried very hard to make amends. The friendly campsite manager
loaded me with advice and bus tickets; while at the tourist office in the centre
of town a very sweet lady, her eyes an astonishing shade of green, changed my
sterling out of her own pocket when the exchange clerk failed to return from
lunch.

Budapest turns its best face to the river. For most of its history it has
consisted of the rival towns of Buda and Pest, glaring at each other across the
Danube. The two were not even linked by bridge until the beginning of the last
century, and finally amalgamated only in 1873. Consequently the single city
possesses a double ration of imposing waterfront architecture; although
topography gives the Buda side, on the west, the advantage of two spectacular
citadels.

There is now a line of bridges. Oldest and most splendid is the Chain
Bridge, whose roadway passes under great towers at each end before diving
straight under the Castle Hill. Alongside the tunnel entrance is a funicular
railway, by which I rode effortlessly to the top. The view on the way was all I'd
expected, and more.

This is the largest of the central European citadels, with room for wide roads, shops, restaurants, and even hotels; bottom marks went to the Budapest Hilton, a vulgar monstrosity in concrete and brown glass. The Mátyás Church, unfortunately next door, was in stark contrast. Its exterior style is very similar to that of Vienna - not surprising, considering half a century of cultural exchanges under the Austro-Hungarian Empire. Quite small, light and elegant as a piece of fine porcelain, it has a single, asymmetrically placed Gothic tower of the most delicate stonework over a roof patterned with red, green and ochre tiles.

Every inch of the interior is decorated with colour of some kind: nineteenth century frescoes, gilded statuary, stained glass shedding rainbow light on the chapels down each side. That of King Béla III contained a chamber organ with a huge number of pipes, some so slender that you would hardly dare to blow wind through them. Impossible to believe, breathing the air exhaled by years of Holy Church, that under the Ottoman Turks this site was once a mosque.

Outside is an equestrian statue to King Stephen, the tenth century hero who welded the Magyars into a single state. All around him the square was full of idlers, crowding the stalls of the vendors or just strolling in the sun. A couple of players, not quite far enough apart, were busking on accordions, and I heard at least one familiar Hungarian dance.

This is the centre of gravity of Castle Hill, and around it is the Hill's most striking feature. The Fishermen's Bastion, named for its position overlooking the Watertown on the Danube bank below, was compared in the guide book to a drawing by Esher. It was the perfect description: a compound of The Belvedere with the pillars and stairways of Ascending and Descending. Steps and promenades, the lower levels looking through arches on to the river, connect seven three-tiered, conical turrets: one for each of the seven Magyar tribes who came out of Central Asia, bringing their horses and their Turkic language with them, to settle the land eleven hundred years ago.

I sat and recharged my batteries on one of the towers, enjoying surely the best view to be had of the city spread out below. A steep flight of steps took me down into the fishermen's quarter of the Watertown, and between fine old houses, some incongruously topped with television aerials.

The square at the bottom was a bus terminus, but my homeward one wasn't there. So I made for the metro, dodging among headscarved ladies selling flowers of all descriptions. Among the usual daffodils and irises were fresh-picked bluebells and anemonies, bringing a whiff of country air to downtown Budapest.

Nineteen forints was a ridiculous amount of change to find, especially as the ticket machine spat out my twenty forint piece with disgust. So I travelled on my bus ticket with the simple excuse ready, if challenged, that I "didn't know" it should be specially stamped. A small deception, and one I performed shamelessly. For I was still distinctly out of humour with all things Hungarian.

Try as I might to distract myself from the events of the previous night, they accompanied me every step of the way, leaving me profoundly depressed. The whole country seemed diminished. Every Hungarian on the street was inimical, every policeman a potential monster.

Back at the campsite, someone had anticipated me by fixing a long hose to the tap. Unfortunately, I got talking to another couple while my tank filled, and flooded the van before I could turn it off. No harm done; a little careful manoeuvring on to a handy bump made for a well-angled tilt. By the time I had returned from my own soaking under a blissfully hot shower, it was draining nicely.

*

Water could have been my theme for Budapest.

The hot mineral springs of the area have been enjoyed since Roman times for their curative and restorative properties. There are many throughout the city, and some whose architecture dates back four hundred years to Ottoman rule. Anything with healing properties seemed too good to miss, so I set off for the Lukács baths to be duly cured and restored.

The attendant gave me a towel and token, locked up my clothes and pointed me in the right direction. I found myself in a pillared hall with four pools: 32°, 36°, 40°C respectively, plus a cold plunge of 24°. Most of the bathers were sitting round the edges talking, for all but one pool were too small for real swimming. Rather, you are supposed to soak away your troubles for an hour or so, in a pleasantly social atmosphere.

Fine if you go with friends, or can speak Hungarian. I splashed around in each pool, all in the wrong order, and swam a little in the largest. Soon I was getting bored. The sulphurous smell was overpowering, like being inside a gigantic, slightly rotten egg. So I finished up with a cold plunge and a long shower. I didn't want the smell following me all the way to the Baltic.

The attendant was crestfallen and openly disapproving to see me back so soon. I soothed him with compliments and the excuse that time pressed. All the same I felt steamy and wrinkled for the rest of the day, having had more water in the last twenty-four hours than in the whole previous fortnight.

*

Budapest Zoo used to be a breeding centre for the Przewalski Horse, and as such deserved a visit.

It occupies a corner of the Városliget, or City Park, several acres of pleasure gardens to the east of the city centre. There was the usual collection of drably confined, depressed animals, though the rather more imaginative concrete mountain at its centre, built in 1866 to house the star exhibits, was then far ahead of its time.

As for the Przewalskis, it was a disappointment. The enclosure marked on the map with a horse - predictably the furthest pen - turned out to contain a Shetland pony!

But it was worth going, just to see the elephant. Separated from the public by a set of wicked-looking spikes around his pen, he performed a circus balancing act over them, stretching to the limit of his trunk for apples and biscuits. The zoo's strangest exhibit, at any rate to one coming from an island of north-west Europe, was a cage of common seagulls. The sound of their cries was disconcerting, heard over a central European suburb.

I could still hear them from outside the zoo, mixed with the honking and quacking from the lake, where families were feeding the ducks. The weather had suddenly turned very hot, and it seemed as if half Budapest had come out in its shirtsleeves to cool down with leisure and ice-cream, or by going for a paddle.

In the middle of the park is Hösök Tere, the Heroes' Square. By name and nature it seems typically Communist, a setting for massed Party rallies and rousing, worthy speeches. In fact it was laid out a century ago, and the figure on the tall central column is not Lenin but Gabriel. Below him is a mounted guard of Magyar chieftains; behind, two curving colonnades enthrone fourteen more Hungarian kings.

Here, in Hösök Tere, Imre Nagy was ceremonially re-interred in 1989, a gesture symbolic of throwing off the Communist yoke. Nagy, architect of the liberal reforms which led to the Hungarian Uprising in 1956, was less fortunate than his Czech counterpart Dubček, for the Russians hanged him as a traitor.

Today, most of the square was lifeless and almost deserted. A docile herd of tourists shuffled in one corner, obedient to the directions of their guide. The assembled ranks of Hungarian kings were draped in an assortment of teenage girls, looking on with elaborate boredom while their young men, wearing only sawn-off jeans and rollerblades, showed off their skills on the parade-ground smoothness of the paving stones.

*

Yet another long, hot shower, and I was almost ready to go. I filled up my last water container from the same tap as before, only to find the water a murky grey and smelling of diesel. It was so badly contaminated I had to ditch the bottle too. This was potential bad news, as I already had five gallons of the stuff from the day before. I drove off without checking it. Sufficient unto the day...

Absorbed in a good worry, I became dimly aware that heads were turning as the van passed. Good for them. I was proud of the smart little vehicle, and it was nice that others shared the opinion. Feeling unreasonably pleased, I came round a bend to find myself head-on to another car on the left-hand side of the road. I rapidly got a grip on myself and the wheel, and swerved back on to my own side, after which public interest abruptly disappeared.

Postponing the plunge into Budapest's traffic, I took a detour round the Buda Hills. The road rambled dizzily around hillsides, their covering of beech and wild cherry just breaking into leaf. But for the chairlift briefly overhead and rack railway alongside, you wouldn't have believed that this was only half-an-hour from the centre of a capital city. There are said to be wild boar here, among an abundance of other wildlife.

Back in the city, the traffic was a nightmare, the complex one-way system even worse. It bore me alternately north and south in slow fits and starts, forbidding me to turn left or right although all I wanted was to go east. When at last the city spat me out, it was into an early weekend crawl that choked the roads for miles.

At last there was the option of a route on minor roads. The saving in distance would be very little, and the roads themselves of dubious quality; but nothing could be slower than the journey so far. I decided that if the first turn-off was anything more than just a cart-track, I'd take it.

It was a gamble that paid dividends. For this was now the fringe of the Great Hungarian Plain. With no obstacles to avoid, no need to humour the lie of the land, the country lane ran as straight as a die. I could bowl along at sixty with little interruption.

The first village, Kunhegyes, was a gem of pastel-pink almond blossom interspersed with white damson and blackthorn. At the far end was a lemon-yellow church. It was as if a giant had scattered dolly-mixture. From now on one attractive village succeeded another, and Budapest might have been a thousand miles away.

The common prefix, "Kun...", gave a clue to the local history. It is a contraction of Kuman, the name of a Turkic people who once occupied southern Russia, known as Polovtsi to the Russians - and Borodin*. Fleeing

* As in the "Polovtsian Dances" of the opera "Prince Igor"

westwards before the advancing Mongols, they offered their swords to the Hungarian king in return for lands to settle here.

In between their villages were farmsteads; long, low buildings of whitewash topped by red tiles. They were at once cosy and functional, while usually slightly down-at-heel. Feeling the pinch, perhaps.

Hungary's agriculture is in an uncomfortable state of flux. Nothing unusual in the farming world these days; the same might be said of most of Europe. But then, that is part of the problem.

The idea of collective farms was abandoned with Communism itself, and since then stock numbers have dropped considerably. The East European markets have dwindled, and Hungary is looking more to the West to sell its produce. Unfortunately, the European Union's predilection for mobile goalposts hurts more than just its own farmers.

Sudden import bans on quarantine grounds, sudden changes in fruit prices, are only small examples of an unpredictable situation. Meanwhile the EU is happy to dump its surplus on Hungary at heavily subsidised prices; while the country's own agricultural subsidies are among the lowest in the world. Life can rarely have been harder for Hungarian farmers. How can they move with the times, when the times themselves don't know where they are moving from one day to the next?

By contrast Hortobágy, where I was now heading, is in something of a time warp. In its 630 square kilometres of National Park, old customs and methods are lovingly preserved for public interest. The whims of Brussels, the loss of the Soviet markets, mean little inside the comfortable embrace of Hortobágy's borders.

The miles now dropped away at colossal speed, and the earlier heavy showers were giving way to golden evening sunshine. My clouds of depression were simultaneously lifting, and at last I began to feel more at one with Hungary.

Towards the end of the journey, the hedges disappeared to show great tracts of open country. Among the farm buildings, strange lever-balance structures gave sharp silhouettes against the sunset. Here and there sheafs of reeds were piled high in oversized stooks.

Then the turning for Hortobágy was upon me with a suddenness that called for a violent swerve, and I reached the village just in time to be still able to see it.

CHAPTER VIII: HUNGARY'S WILD WEST

Four legs good, two legs bad

(George Orwell: Animal Farm)

The Great Hungarian Plain, or Puszta, is the geographical and spiritual heartland of Hungary. Its grasslands once covered half the surface of the country, from the borders with Romania and Ukraine in the east, to where the Danube flows into Slovenia due south of Budapest.

Today, much of its acreage has been turned into arable land. But in some places, notably Hortobágy's National Park, you can catch a strong whiff of the lifestyle and culture which, a hundred years ago, set the Puszta mid-way between the Steppes of Central Asia and the American Wild West.

Hortobágy is a living museum. Here the ancient breeds of cattle and sheep are lovingly nurtured, and the Magyar horsemen still hone their rough-riding skills. Here, too, is one of the two State Studs of Noniusz horses, the breed that was once the mainstay of Hungary's agriculture - and, in an earlier age, of its cavalry. And here the famous Bridge Fair is still held every July, which for a couple of centuries has drawn the best of the riders for two intensive days of markets and rodeos.

Around Hortobágy, the horse is supreme. Simply, it is the best, indeed the only, way to get about; for motor vehicles are banned from leaving the few metalled roads. They would, in any case, for much of the year be impractical on the boggy surface.

That suited me very nicely. Much as I appreciated the little van, it would make a nice change to exchange driving seat for saddle, and explore the Plain in the time-honoured way.

*

At the tiny village of Máta, just outside Hortobágy, the new Epona Hotel and Rider Village form a late twentieth century island in an early nineteenth century green sea.

The hotel, only a year old, illustrates the strength of the Capitalist surge following the demise of Communism. Its focus, indeed its raison d'être, is the horse, and its location is due to the presence at Máta of the State Noniusz Stud and Riding School. There is also a growing private side to the stables, and nowadays about half the horses here are kept for showjumping and dressage.

The two are inter-dependent faces of the same coin. The riding facilities bring custom to the hotel, which offers self-contained accommodation with stabling for a visitor's own horse; while the guests of the hotel support the state venture by hiring from the Riding School, or joining one of the regular wagon trips out into the Plain.

Here, for the first time, I was expected, having laid my plans in advance. The manager, Ildiko Koti, was a slight, dark lady in her twenties who spoke faultless English. The first morning she kindly gave up an hour to show me around the complex. We began with the Epona itself then moved on via the Rider Village - a set of self-contained units catering for four people and one or two horses - to the enormous complex of the Riding School.

The horses were stalled in long, low barns, whose corners were thick with the dust of centuries. Hundreds of swallows flew among the rafters, swooping and diving between the sunbeams that angled through every crack.

There is stabling here for well over a hundred horses. About half of these are Noniusz geldings, the surplus from the stud, which are kept for the use of visiting dudes. It was as one of these that I was introduced to Bogar, a tough-looking dark bay with a wicked gleam in his eye. "The name," Ildiko told me with a similar gleam, "means 'Bug'."

Now came the bad news. I was to be tested in the schooling arena for competence before being allowed out on to the open spaces of the Puszta. I had explained about my illness, as a precaution against being given a strong or excitable horse; nowadays I don't "ride", so much as sit on top as a passenger. This is fine for riding out, using a horse as a pleasant vehicle and covering up to ten times the ground that I could manage on foot. But school work, involving riding figures in a controlled way with changes of pace, is physically demanding. I couldn't afford to wobble. To be "spun" at this stage would be unbearable.

The first bit was the worst: getting on. It would hardly make a good impression if I had to be shovelled into the saddle by a team of weightlifters. Fortunately Bogar was small, and I made it fairly respectably. After a mercifully short five minutes of walking and trotting circles with one brief canter, I was certified safe. The lad who was to accompany me failed his own test by forgetting to tighten his girth before getting up. It made his attempt to mount rather more painful than mine had been.

Directly behind the stables was a copse. The sound of birdsong followed us for the length of a railed paddock housing the Noniusz mares and foals. But within a hundred yards we were away from all let or hindrance, with only the occasional farmstead to break up the flat surface as far as the eye could see.

A feeling of perfect liberation washed over me. With no barriers to stop me, no road to be kept to and four good legs underneath me, I could go as I liked without the aid of mechanisation or tarmac. When my companion, sensing my mood or just looking at my face, said, "Faster?" I wasn't inclined to disagree.

That was his one word of English, and one more than my Hungarian. No matter; here there was no need of conversation. Yet I was glad of his company, for after a mile or two I was completely disorientated by the uniformity.

Although in fact it wasn't uniform at all, for every two or three miles a few trees rose out of the flatness to give shape briefly back to the landscape. Here and there, more frequent than the sparse farm buildings, we came upon a well, visible from afar by the outline of the counterpoise system through which water is raised - like an Egyptian *shaduf.* That each of these wells has its own name is a mark of their importance. A hundred years ago the herdsmen of the Puszta knew them all intimately, using them for navigation.

Riding up for a closer look at one, I found it surprisingly shallow, with the water only about ten feet down. There was water lying extensively on the surface, too, evidence of heavy winter rains. It wasn't going to be there for long. Summer had arrived with a sudden heatwave, and the pools were almost visibly shrinking.

For now, however, they were the haunt of waterfowl and waders. Egrets and golden plovers paddled on the fringes; all about them lapwings performed joyful aerobatics, each whooping "peewit" call tailing off in a curious corkscrew gurgle. High overhead, the skylarks wove an infinite curtain of song.

There were animals in plenty, too. One or two herds of sheep in the distance; and on the horizon, getting nearer, the main Noniusz herd which we were seeking. Only the nursing mares and the riding horses are kept at Máta. The rest - youngsters, barren mares and the surplus stock - live as they have always done, roaming the plains.

It was none too soon when we reached them. My saddle didn't fit me, and I was suffering. It was a pleasant relief to sit a while watching the sun play on fifty bay coats, their wearers enjoying the first flush of spring grass.

On the way home I was reduced to shortening my stirrups to alter the fall of weight; harder work for the legs but some relief for my blisters. Even so, by the time we returned to the stables, I was experiencing the common complaint of dudes since time immemorial: a very sore bottom.

A mile out of Hortobágy village was the airfield. Actually it just looked like another bit of the Puszta, but a small aeroplane stood by to prove its credentials.

From here a former airline pilot runs his own one-man company, taking tourists on air safaris in a couple of 1944 Antonov-2 biplanes leased from Aeroflot. To my disappointment he had just taken off on an evening sunset flight; but the elderly man who was keeping an eye on things in his absence invited me aboard his spare plane to look around.

The little plane was battered and dented, its nose apparently patched with cardboard. As I climbed off the stepladder into the fuselage it creaked complainingly. Inside, though, the dozen or so seats looked invitingly comfortable, if rather moth-eaten. In spite of my doubts about anything Aeroflot had chucked out, I signed up enthusiastically for next day's flight.

A few miles further, past the village of Halastó, are the lakes now known as the fishponds. Although these look natural, they are really artificial, dating from the early 1900s; their subsequent use for fish rearing gave them their present name. They are famous for their bird life, which includes storks, egrets and spoonbill cranes.

Halastó itself wasn't attractive. Its run-down houses were approached over a main street that was mostly mud. Geese squelched around, honking noisily. Hard alongside stood rows of pigsties, equally muddy; while behind there were ditches, full of stagnant, stinking water, cutting the houses off from the lakes themselves. At least the swallows liked it. There must have been several thousand wheeling about overhead.

Fruitlessly casting around for a way to cross the ditches, I was about to give up when a small, grizzled man came across to give me some friendly help. He led me round the barns to where a bridge was hiding, and with a wave saw me across and on to the bank by the water.

From here, you could see the artificial nature of the lakes. A six-foot bank enclosed them; along its top a road ran straight as a die back towards Hortobágy, of which a few knobs were just visible in the sunset haze.

But my attention was riveted on the water, throbbing and pulsating with thousands of birds. Overhead, ducks and geese departed for their evening roosts in a constant to-and-fro. The reeds fringing the track were full of sedge warblers. And there was another noise that swamped even that of the waterfowl: the croaking of innumerable frogs. Before me ran a bow-wave of splashes, as they dived at the approach of footsteps.

A high, crooning sound filled the background. Strangely insubstantial, it defied any effort to get closer to its source, seeming to retreat before me and close in behind. In the red evening light, it lent a spooky feel to the scene. It would hardly have been surprising if a hand had risen from the lake brandishing a sword.

A little way along stood a rickety observation tower. I climbed it and sat writing up my diary, fending off hordes of ravening mosquitoes. Just as the sun disappeared the little biplane came over the horizon, and I watched it pass overhead and continue all the way to a safe landing on the distant airstrip. Tomorrow I would be up there inside it.

*

But there was disappointment in store. Although yesterday had been busy, today I was the only customer. Without five more of me, the trip was off. The pilot, a dark, good-looking man who reminded me irresistibly of Caligula in the BBC's "I Claudius", had abandoned his flying cap and goggles to lounge in swimming trunks under the hot sun.

For already, in April, the temperature was in the high eighties, and the infamous mirages of the Hortobágy plains were winding themselves up for their full summer tricks. Yet the trees were still bare, the grass only just sprouting. Evidently spring is almost non-existent here, with summer following immediately on the heels of winter.

Back in Hortobágy, a crop of early tourists were spilling out of their coaches, to disperse among the vendors' stalls lining the main street. These sold a variety of local goods and souvenirs: fine lacework and embroidery, reed basketry, sheepskins and leather goods. The last were the most varied and numerous, including everything imaginable from tourist kitsch to functional items such as water bottles and stockwhips. In olden times, these whips were used by stockmen for killing wolves, each kill being recorded with a notch on the handle. These days, in the hands of an enthusiastic townie, they are more likely to decapitate an innocent bystander.

It was cooler and safer inside the Shepherds' Museum. Here, commentaries in four languages - Hungarian, Russian, German and English - described the past life on the plains.

Life wasn't all whips, wolves and wells for the herdsmen. Among the cooking pots and branding irons were exhibits from a sophisticated culture. The embroidered felt and woollen clothing was brilliant in colour and complex in design, with different costumes assigned to the different classes. Among the cowbells were delicate zithers, one with a beautiful scroll carved into a horse's head.

Just outside, the Epona Hotel had its own exhibition stall. "Our staff are always at your stable," said the poster on the front, "ready to satisfy even extraordinary demands."

So they were. István Soós, the resident vet, generously spent a couple of hours showing me round the stud farm. He explained how the company which had built the hotel last year had also leased the entire stable complex from the state. Under the agreement it assumed sole responsibility for the Noniusz herd, in return for the facilities used in setting up the private Equestrian Centre.

The Noniusz he described as "Rough, tough, able to go all day but with a mind of its own". The breed originated from a stallion captured by Austrian soldiers from Napoleonic troops at the beginning of the nineteenth century. Himself called Noniusz, the horse was so prized at the military stud that he was used on his own daughters in a frenzy of inbreeding.

For a hundred years his descendants were mainly cavalry horses. Thereafter, with changing times, they became widely used in agriculture, where their combination of strength with athleticism made them more highly regarded than the average draught animal.

Fifties mechanisation ousted the Noniusz. The breed might have died out; but the State stepped in to preserve it as a piece of history, establishing studs here, and at Mezőhegyes in the south. Currently there are about two hundred horses on the two sites.

István took me to see the stallion, Mako. At 16.3 hands he was unusually big, his marked Roman nose and massive neck contributing to the overall appearance of solidity and colossal power. A black, he stood out among Hortobágy's long lines of bays; for he was brought from Mezőhegyes. "They breed black for preference there," István explained.

"Why doesn't his door have a nameplate, like all the others?"

" 'Mako' is only a stable name," he said. "Officially, he's "Noniusz 33"!' A numbers-only system for stallions, he added, had been military custom dating from the Turkish wars. The method is further complicated by returning to zero every time the fiftieth sire is reached - which must confuse the stud book no end!

We had now reached the end of the Noniusz barns, and István took me through the blacksmith's shop into his inner sanctum, the small office and surgery that were his own private domain. As we chatted of this and that, I told him about my own horses while he told me about some of his more unusual cases. His position here was only as old as the hotel - one year - and there was an air of compulsive enthusiasm about him as he described how he planned to extend the scope of his work. "People here," he said, "work hard and play hard." It was clear that István meant to concentrate on the first.

Outside, by the huge training arena, we sat to watch dressage enthusiast Agnes Borsó schooling a superb black stallion, Kaszarda, in counter-canter and flying changes. He had been bred here, I learned, by a resident stallion imported from Germany.

Hortobágy occupies a central position in Hungary's equestrian calendar. The annual International Jumping Show, held here every June, draws competitors from all over Europe. With standards like these to aim for, Hortobágy's breeders have no time for the humble Noniusz. Blood must be blue; and preferably German.

But not, as I immediately asked, Hanoverian. The breed beloved of German showjumpers doesn't appeal to the Hungarians. It needed too much to be dominated, explained István; to be ridden with Germanic precision that told it exactly where to place each of its feet and when. His own countrymen preferred a horse that could think for itself a bit. That was where the Holstein came in. His eyes gleamed. Here, I suddenly felt, we had got to the centre of things, the place where István's heart lay.

It was a challenge he relished, he said, to raise horses from stallions bred to a different kind of climate. "You have the same genes," he said, "But the result can be totally different. For one thing, it's possible to produce a much tougher horse." Here, he would be able to observe over a long period the results of raising German Holstein stock to the harsher, more extreme conditions of the eastern Hungarian Plain.

Agnes had finished with Kaszarda. Covered with sweat from working under the hot sun, he was led away for the equine equivalent of a shower: a long, cooling session with a hosepipe. Afterwards she brought out a magnificent white stallion, like an oversized Lippizaner. Summás was an Intermediate Dressage horse. I watched spellbound as Agnes took him through his repertoire with consummate ease; and then began to teach him the Piaffe and Passage, two versions of the elegant, high-stepping Spanish Walk of Haute École dressage.

He couldn't quite get it right. He was, after all, only learning; but Agnes was disparaging. He wouldn't, she thought, make the Grand Prix grade he was aimed for. Meanwhile, István was getting bored. Would I like to see the Holstein stallion he had brought from Germany to do a stud season here?

He led me to the stable of one of the "Rider Houses" attached to the Epona.

Here, with enormous pride, he introduced me to Larinero, half a ton of gleaming bay muscle and bone leased at a high premium.

Was he worth it, I wondered? "He'll get both showjumpers and dressage horses," said István, "and in his year here he'll serve a hundred and fifty mares." My jaw dropped: nearly four times the usual number.

"Artificial insemination," explained István laconically. Pointing to a plastic covered contraption like a vaulting horse, he added, "That's our dummy."

Poor Larinero. A hundred and fifty nubile Hungarian fillies awaiting his attentions, and he had to act out his romantic fantasies on a plastic inflatable. But that's private enterprise for you.

*

When it comes to pulling a heavy covered wagon full of tourists over the mud and ruts of the Puszta, the "rough, tough" Noniusz has the Holstein sewn up any day.

These trips give the non-rider a taste of the plains, together with a close look at some living history. Since neither my posterior, nor any other part of me, was equal to another ride just yet, I signed up to join one.

The sun was burning down again, and I sat waiting with the group in the shelter of the stable wall, watching the antics of a stork on its nest at the top of a telegraph pole. Nightingales in the nearby copse were singing their hearts out; while away in the dressage arena, Summás was making a better job of his Piaffe today. In the far distance I could just make out Caligula's planes, still firmly grounded.

At last the wagons arrived. The driver of one was my friend from Halastó. The group included an Australian couple, the husband of Hungarian origin and back on holiday to visit his family. He chatted bilingually throughout, with his wife on the one hand and his brother and cousins on the other. Very useful; he was able to translate the driver's commentary for his wife, and allowed me to listen in.

The tour was a cultural and agricultural odyssey. Rumbling off at a steady trot, we left the stables via a corral of Noniusz youngstock. A white-flowered hedge bordered their paddock, and its gloriously sweet scent drifted through the wagon and lingered for a hundred yards. Almost immediately we were on to the Puszta, and heading for a couple of long, low, reed-thatched farm buildings.

Halting in the centre of the farmyard beside the inevitable well, the driver invited us to dismount. A strong smell of sheep came from the barns, and we looked inside to find them tightly crammed, literally heaving, with half-grown lambs. These were the famous Racka sheep, one of the rare breeds carefully cherished by the National Park.

On the grassland nearby were their parents. With shaggy coats and grotesquely twisted horns, they appeared only half domesticated, a throwback to wild and woolly ancestors from some forgotten era. Racka sheep used to be kept for their milk as much as their meat. This is still used to make Gomolya cheese, similar to Rocquefort. The fleeces - always white or black - are also used. "If you see a grey Racka," Ildiko had said, "it's just getting on a bit!"

As the journey resumed, the driver told us a little of past life on the plains. There have been settlements here since prehistoric times; but Hungarian history is usually reckoned to have begun with the arrival of the Magyar tribes at the end of the ninth century.

Storming out of Central Asia like so many before them, the Magyar horsemen were wrongly identified by the West with their Hun predecessors, an error perpetuated by the name of Hungary that subsequently clung to their land. The Hungarians themselves call it Magyarország.

Their possession of the Hortobágy area was constantly disrupted. The Magyars were first driven out by the Mongols of the so-called Golden Horde, whose relentless westward thrust under their leader, Batu, had brought them through Russia and Poland and into Hungary. In 1241 the Mongols took Pest and were soon knocking on the gates of Vienna. Western history might have been very different, but for news that came suddenly galloping out of Mongolia: the Great Khan had died. Now Batu had bigger fish to fry. Himself a candidate for the hotly disputed succession, he soon forgot his diversion among tiny countries at the wrong end of the world. The invasion was abandoned.

In its wake the Magyars drifted slowly back, only to be expelled a couple of centuries later by the Ottoman Turks. Under the hundred and fifty years of Turkish occupation, the land reverted to uncultivated wasteland. It was now that the plains acquired the label of "Puszta", meaning "deserted, waste".

New settlers cleared the forests and drained the marshes for agriculture. However, without the protection of the trees, frequent and heavy flooding ensued which gradually carried off the topsoil. Left unsuitable for crops, the land was given over to grazing. In time, the plains came to resemble the prairies of the American mid-west.

And now began the most colourful era of the Puszta. Around the sheep and cattle grew up the culture of the herdsmen, a cowboy lifestyle that was to last for over a hundred years.

These men belonged to a society governed by a strict hierarchy, whose prestige peaked with the *csikós* - horsemen - declining through the cattlemen and shepherds, to the lowly swineherd at the bottom of the ladder. Spending months at a time away from their families, they navigated the uniform green sea via the wells. At night they cooked and slept in reed shelters like wigwams, whose Magyar name translates as "sitting on its backside".

With the early part of this century, increasing mechanisation saw more and more of the Plain falling under cultivation. The new arable land was parcelled into collectives when Communism took hold after the war. With the transformation of most of its people from cowboy to *kolkhoznik*, the culture of the Puszta seemed doomed.

It was the infertility of its ground that preserved Hortobágy. Its grudging subsoil, prodigal only of grass, refused any other crop. In the fifties, the Communist administration even tried to turn it into paddy fields to grow rice; but the Party moguls had not done their homework, and the attempt was a miserable failure. The people of Hortobágy might bend to Party ideology, but its land remained obdurate.

And so a fragment of plains culture survived, a spark fanned by the establishment of the National Park. And if the Racka sheep are an anachronism, the grey horned cattle preserved as a biological curiosity, and the cowboys effectively civil servants, who cares?

Certainly the rough-riding skills of the latter are sharp as ever. As we approached the Noniusz herd, we saw galloping towards us the daredevil acrobat of the "Koch-5". He drove at breakneck speed a team of five horses harnessed three and two, himself standing with one foot on each rump of the rear two.

This circus act originated not on the Plain, but in the mind of an Austrian artist who painted the scene from his imagination. It fired the bravado of the csikós; "If he can think of it, we can do it!" they cried, and proceeded to make good the boast. Yet even among these hard men, very few could manage the trick. It remains a skill handed from father to son.

The nineteen-year-old lad performing for us had learned it from his father, as he had from his. Without a wobble he circled us twice and then, slipping down to sit astride one of the horses, came to a halt in front of us, one lead horse theatrically pawing the ground.

His three companions, wearing like him traditional costume of blue shirt, black breeches and hat with upswept brim, followed with a display of the complete trust and obedience of their horses. Dismounting, they brought them to a sitting position, which the horses maintained unmoving while the riders cracked whips over their heads. Then, removing the felt saddles, they urged the horses to lie full length while the men stood literally on top of them, still cracking their whips.

Now came the most dramatic bit. The csikós replaced the saddles and leapt on with barely a touch to the stirrup - for, unbelievably, their saddles have no girth. Now they gathered the Noniusz herd, which stood nearby shuffling and stamping uneasily. Shouting and cracking their stockwhips, they urged the horses into a gallop, and drove them three times, with tight control, around our little group. The drumming of hooves, the yelling and cracking of whips, drowned even the constant song of the skylarks, and the smell of hot horse vied with the dust in our lungs.

After such a rodeo display, anything more was bound to be an anti-climax. But there was a timeless quality about the herd of grey cattle, moving slowly over the grass to the accompaniment of bleating calves and rattling cowbells.

These cattle, long-haired and terrifyingly horned, are more representative of the Puszta than any other animal. Of ancient bloodline and primitive appearance, they bear a marked resemblance to the aurochs, the proto-cow which became extinct only a few hundred years ago.

Their calves are of a striking golden colour, fit to gladden the hearts of the apostate children of Israel. At three months or thereabouts, they turn the dull grey that will last the rest of their lives. The breed makes for poor milkers. Formerly they were used mainly for draught work, and for their excellent beef. Today, however, they run no risk of being eaten; they are protected at Hortobágy, as elsewhere, to maintain the genetic bank.

At last it was time to head for home over the flat, grassy plain with its many muddy ruts, pausing to give the horses a long drink at one of the wells.

Back in Hortobágy, the stables were shimmering in the heat. It was too hot to rest in the van, so I took a pillow into the copse, to drowse in the shade for a few hours and listen to the nightingales.

By late afternoon, the temperature was more bearable. I said some goodbyes, and hit the road.

CHAPTER IX: AIRS ABOVE GROUND - AND BELOW

And they said, "Speak to us of beauty." And he
answered, "...the restless have heard her shouting
among the mountains; and with her voice came the
drumming of hooves, and the beating of wings..."

(Jibran Khalil Jibran: The Prophet)

From the map, the next section promised infinite variety. My route led westward through the Plains to cross the marshes of the River Tisza at Tiszafüred; then north into the hills to reach the tiny village of Szilvásvárad on the edge of the Bükk mountains.

At first the scenery changed only gradually, with the endless sea of grass giving place to the odd patch of turned soil and rather more trees. Another few miles, and nearly all the land was under the plough, showing a strikingly rich, dark earth in dramatic contrast with the green and gold of the newly fledged poplars. Was this where all Hortobágy's topsoil had ended up?

It took a fair time to cross the wetlands around Tiszafüred. Second only to the Danube among Hungary's rivers, the Tisza rises in the Ukrainian Carpathians and wobbles its drunken way almost the length and breadth of Hungary, dropping an oxbow here and a swamp there, before wriggling out of the country to the south and emptying itself into the Danube just above Belgrade. Beyond it, a blue ridge of mountains - the Bükk - was still only a suggestion in the hazy distance.

Between the two lay glorious country, a gently rolling downland with tight little patches of cultivation, mainly vines and orchards on south facing slopes. The hedges and thickets rioted with blossom: more blackthorn than I had ever seen, and much of the sweet-scented thorn common at Hortobágy. And they were thick with nightingales. More than once, on stopping for a map-check, I was treated to a concert performance through the open window from only a few feet away.

My planned route lay straight over the top of the Bükk, but the road, although well-graded on the map, deteriorated into a cart-track. I gave it half a mile, then turned back. This was frustrating, as it meant a back-track to the village of Bogacs, and then a detour round three sides of a square through Eger and other tedious industrial towns. Moreover, it was now getting late.

But the evening, and the countryside, were compensation. As I drove westward over the undulating road the sun was directly ahead. It set, then rose, then set again, as suns tend to do among mountains; it was as if it kept popping its head over the next hill to check that I was following. Eger was at first pinkly attractive and fringed with vineyards, source of the infamous "Bull's Blood" wine; then beset by a uniformity of high-rise flats, and depressing.

Beyond, the road plunged between crags and followed a rapid stream sharply uphill for some miles, to emerge at Monosbel under an extraordinary white, naked-looking mountain. On a closer look this strange rock-face wasn't, after all, natural; rather, the face of a quarry which had split the mountain from top to toe. It was that time of dusk for trompe-l'oeil; a knobbly castle a mile ahead on the main road turned into an industrial monstrosity as the headlights stripped away its pretences.

A couple more miles, and I came into Szilvásvárad just as the last of the light slid behind the Slovakian mountains.

*

A park ranger jerked me too abruptly into the following day. It appeared that the Bükk National Park began on the outskirts of the village, and the ordinary-looking patch of grass on which I had gratefully flaked out in yesterday's darkness was part of it. I apologised and moved away to a car park, to put in a further couple of hours' recharging; then shared my breakfast with a greedy nuthatch, and set out to look around.

The bait which had lured me to Szilvásvárad was the Hungarian State Stud Farm of Lippizaners, the magnificent white horses of Spanish origin bred for four hundred years in Austria and trained for Haut École, or High School Dressage, at the Spanish Riding School in Vienna. Their cousins here were in some sort political exiles, for the receding tide of the Austro-Hungarian Empire had left the Stud behind, like a piece of flotsam, three-quarters of a century ago.

Life in Szilvásvárad revolves around horses. Almost immediately I came upon the indoor competition arena, now, out of season, deserted. A few yards away was the Lippizaner Museum, also silent, for today was Sunday. I stopped to ask my way, and while I stood in the road, a farm cart rumbled by... drawn by two Lippizaners! I was momentarily scandalised. Had the people here no respect for the quality of these animals? Unfortunately, as I later learned, this was to some extent the case.

I drove out of the town and made a circuit of it before finally finding the main riding school. Not a horse was in sight. The only signs of life emanated faintly from a toothless old man hosing some flowers. He pointed me to the manager's office, where I could arrange to ride the next day.

I had intended admitting to my illness. But the manager spoke no English and only a little German, and conversation was monosyllabic and awkward. I feared to be misunderstood; and to be horsed on some old riding school plug among these blue-blooded, almost mythical creatures would break my heart.

In any case, I reasoned, a slow horse needing to be constantly, physically urged on is hard work, and would finish me off in five minutes. I had managed at Hortobágy, and this of all occasions must not be spoiled. I held my tongue and crossed my fingers - and the next day was magnificently rewarded.

Stopping only to buy a straw hat against the intensifying sun, I headed for the hills for the rest of the day. The road climbed, twisted, climbed, backtracked above itself and climbed some more. At last from an outcrop I looked down directly on the town far below, watching as from Mount Olympus the distant and trivialised bustle of daily life. There in the middle was the stud farm - attached after all to the riding school, and identifiable by a number of white specks in the field below. I lazed in the warmth, watching the specks climb the hill while the sun climbed the sky, and when the horses disappeared over the other side I scuttled like a lizard into a patch of shade.

"Bükk" means "beech", and the mountains are aptly named. On the lower slopes bloomed wild cherry, rowan and the ubiquitous blackthorn, but up here the beech held court, its bare branches still in the grip of winter. Spring, however, was creeping inexorably up the hillside. In the two days of my stay the green tide-mark moved upwards so fast as to excite local comment; for the temperature reached 28°, exceptional here in late April.

At the top, the road entered a restricted area of the National Park, and was closed to traffic. A pleasantly laid-out picnic area offered a consolation prize to those who had made it thus far. I had it to myself, only a couple of Park Land-Rovers passing all day. At this altitude even the mosquitoes were absent.

When the sun dropped below the trees and the temperature fell like a stone, it was time to head back down... slowly, with frequent stops for the breathtaking views. And another for a traffic jam: with great self-importance, a salamander was walking down the exact centre of the road. Thinking him at first to be a chameleon, I placed him on my yellow file to see whether he would change colour. Of course nothing happened, except that he panicked and started running round in circles. I felt guilty, and placed him safely in the undergrowth. It was, after all, past lighting-up time, and he was illegal traffic, despite the luminous yellow spots on his black coat.

A short detour up the Szalajka Valley, a local beauty spot, led to a pleasant lake and some waterfalls. "Cataracts" gushes the official IBUSZ brochure; but they were small, and mostly made of concrete anyway. There was nothing to rival the scenery of the rest of the day, so I pushed on down into Szilvásvárad to get a closer sight of the horses before they, and I, went to bed.

Too late. They were already tucked up for the night in large barns. But the evening jaunt wasn't wasted. For the hedgerows around were alive with nightingales singing their Vespers. And these nightingales weren't shy. At home, I have crouched furtively in bushes for hours, and never seen so much as a wing-tip; whereas here they disported themselves in full view, extrovert as sparrows.

I watched entranced, and looked forward to listening throughout the night. As with the horses, though, I was disappointed. The creatures of these parts retire early, and it seemed that I was, for once, the last one to stay on its feet.

*

Early next morning, while the nightingales were still sleeping it off, I was introduced to Marcel and Equador, and was mistaken in both.

Marcel was tall, fair and very good-looking. He was chatting in Hungarian to the stud manager, and I assumed that he was the riding school instructor. For a good twenty minutes we discussed the Lippizaners, both growing increasingly puzzled as we did so; I, as he seemed to know little of the Szilvásvárad stud, and he, as to why I should expect him to. It was only when I asked him how long he had worked here that the penny dropped. He was another client, and I was scarlet.

Equador was tall, grey and very good-looking. However, he was clearly not pure Lippizaner, but only one of the half-breeds. For a moment I was disappointed, and envied Marcel his mare, whose straight profile and powerful yet graceful lines showed off her unmixed blood. But from the second my bottom touched the saddle, I learned the error of my ways. Equador was, quite simply, one of the most enjoyable horses I have ridden.

Our real guide was mounted on a sharp little four-year-old stallion, who skittered along with inexhaustible energy and a wide repertoire of sideways leaps. On the few occasions when he was moving in a straight line, he "dished", or threw his front feet out sideways, making him look like a bumptious child trying to dance a highland fling.

Leaving the back streets of the village behind and heading into the hills, we followed a track roughly parallel with my route of the day before, but perhaps a thousand feet below. It snaked and wound through the beeches, giving occasional half-guessed-at glimpses through the new leaves into the valley beneath. The scent of cherry blossom thickly filled the air.

Emerging from the woods, we threaded a maze of tracks in and out of the foothills and around thickets of oak and hazel. Here and there, coloured pegs marked bits of the path. Marcel questioned our escort, and translated that they were gates and hazard markers for the carriage driving championships held here annually in July. Some of the banks looked too precipitous for even a ridden horse. I would have quailed from attacking them with four wheels and sixteen legs together.

We forded a stream and entered a farmyard where dogs, ducks and children all puddled happily together in the mud. Immediately beyond was a good, firm track through fields, and we broke into a long canter. Equador showed a good turn of foot, with a powerful, raking stride that was quite intoxicating. He was also very fit, for he wouldn't have blown a candle out afterwards. More to the point, nor would I; not a big one, anyway. My legs wobbled justifiably, but there was barely a whinge from heart and lungs. As for my bottom, still raw from Bogar's saddle, that was another matter. Just then, I didn't greatly care.

Szilvásvárad had vanished entirely, but on re-crossing the stream we found it hiding behind a small hill. There was a little bar on the way home where we stopped for beer and coke. By now I was more in the mood for champagne, but my throat was so dry I would have been glad of water.

Back at the stables I bid a sad farewell to Equador - how gladly I would have put him on the roof-rack and taken him home with me! - then moved on with Marcel to a nearby bar to continue rehydrating. He told me that he had been to visit the Noniusz stud at Mezőhegyes in the south, and had stopped here briefly on his way home to Germany for the same reason as I: the Lippizaners. His astonishingly fluent Hungarian was explained by a Hungarian parent.

Well lubricated at last, we returned to the stables for a look at the mares and foals. Third time lucky; from my aerial view yesterday I now knew where to find them. I had forgotten, though, that navigation at ground level is a different thing altogether, and anyway they were a good quarter-mile distant. Long before we reached them my legs were dragging and my head whirling, both reminding me that I had already overspent my budget considerably that morning. It didn't help that I had forgotten to eat anything in the last hour or two, or even to change out of my jodhpur boots, which were definitely not made for walking. So I had a cast-iron excuse to lie in the sun for an hour or two, quietly appreciating the sight of these unselfconscious aristocrats against the backdrop of the mountains.

Mares and foals formed a shifting haphazard pattern, like a well-advanced game of chess. You might have supposed that this company of light-grey ladies, with their invariably dark-coloured offspring, were guilty of mass illicit liaison. But it is not deliberately arcane, "in" jargon that describes a white horse as "grey". The truly white horse is albino, and rare. These, like the majority, carry dark pigment, and are born black or dark bay, becoming iron grey with the first few changes of coat and fading to white only as teenagers.

A mounted horseherd kept watch over them. Not a fence was in sight, and anyway this is, par excellence, the country of the horseherd. The horses played wicked games with him, repeatedly dodging past him into the forbidden cornfield. He responded with threats and curses, cracking his whip and rounding them up in a rodeo gallop; before relapsing once more into gloomy torpor, from which Marcel occasionally coaxed him with sporadic conversation.

When the day grew even hotter, one foal after another abandoned the games to thump down on the grass and doze in the sun. I said my goodbyes and trudged back to the van on a piece of lengthening elastic, to force down mouthfuls of carbohydrate that I was almost too tired to swallow; and then followed the foals' example.

*

My final visit was to the Lippizaner museum at the other end of town. This sets out the history and fortunes of the breed from the founding of the original Imperial Stud at Lippiza down to the present day. Unusually, it includes live exhibits, with a row of stalls housing eight horses.

These are the pick of the horses trained locally for coach teams. For traditions here are very much orientated towards driving, rather then dressage. The high profile of the Spanish Riding School in western Europe tends to obscure the fact that the Lippizaner, like so many European breeds, is essentially a dual purpose - that is, ride and drive - animal. It is only the English, whose long traditions of racing and hunting make for exclusive concentration on the ultimate riding horse, who would rather walk than place their best bloodstock between the shafts.

The two horses I had seen harnessed to a farm cart weren't after all so incongruous. Nevertheless, it was difficult to suppress the feeling that the Szilvásvárad Lippizaners, of such fine quality and impeccable ancestry, and

GERMANY Dresden Opera House

CZECH REPUBLIC View of Prague from Hradčany

HUNGARY The Koch-5, Hortbágy

HUNGARY Lippizaner mares and foals, Szilvásvárad

SLOVAKIA Mediaeval walls of Levoča

POLAND Wooden Church, Zakopane

POLAND Warsaw's restored Town Square

POLAND Lake Wigry

LITHUANIA Gediminas' Castle, Trakai

LATVIA Manor House, Straupe

ESTONIA Tallinn city walls and Kiek in de Kök

Baltic sunset

blessed with incomparable surroundings, are less fortunate in their present custodians.

One of the museum "exhibits" bore a great red-raw patch on his shoulder, the worst harness gall I have seen this side of Cairo. Many of the horses at the riding school were also galled, and some actually in quite poor condition. But the worst thing to see was a deep dent in the profile of their faces. A deformity shown to some extent by nearly all the animals here, it had been caused by being stalled for long hours in a headcollar attached to two heavy, downward-pressing chains. My first, though superficial, impression had not been too far from the truth: that the people here had little real concept of what they possessed.

*

There were a few industrial towns to tick off on the way to the caves of Aggtelek, further along the Slovak border. Beyond them was much of the same gentle, intimate country as on the fringes of the Bükk, punctuated by neat, red-tiled villages with brightly coloured churches and yet more blossom, everywhere blossom. The roads were deserted but for the birds, and hoopoes were among the sparrows flying up before my wheels.

I stopped to serve my four hours' "porridge" in an idyllic copse by a stream. Here, besides the now commonplace nightingales, lived a pair of cuckoos. The woods were full of elder, as those near my home, and a warm, full summer smell contrasted with the early-spring livery of the trees. I felt rather homesick and nostalgic, and my mind played with summer images of haymaking, and punting.

Towards Aggtelek, the landscape began to show limestone features: sink-holes, grotesquely eroded gullies and a pitted crag behind the town. The soil changed colour to a bright red marl. Away in the distance a fire raged out of control across several acres of last year's stubble. It was making for a wood, but nobody seemed concerned. The next morning it was out, extinguished perhaps by the dew, leaving one more charred patch to add to the hundreds already around these parts.

A mile out, and well upwind of the fire, I stopped on a patch of meadow beside a small shrine to St. Francis. There was a wood behind, and an irregular sprouting of conifers over the fields, like an ill-planned garden. Just before dark came a four-footed whisper among the leaves, which approached then sheered off from the van and faded away down the hill. Also, once more, cuckoos and nightingales; and I was satisfied, for here at last they sang me to sleep.

*

It was my teeth that woke me up. They were clicking rhythmically as the pounding of my heart made my body vibrate. As I struggled to consciousness, I heartily wished I hadn't bothered. My legs were rubber, someone was moving furniture inside my ribs, and I generally felt as though I had been run over by a Prague tram. My sins were being visited on me; and I was completely unrepentant.

I lay and savoured the last week's fun, and it was worth every ache. Slowly the orchestrated discomforts faded to pianissimo against an own-trumpet obbligato of satisfaction. While I waited for the stagnant blood to start circulating again, I spent the time calculating how long I'd have to wait before the next bout of normal life.

Some time after mid-day I prised myself out of bed and into the driving seat, and made my way to the caves. It wasn't difficult to choose between the one-hour and three-hour tours. By luck a school coach-party arrived just as I was buying my ticket, so the guide was ready to go immediately.

After the problem of the Moravsky caves I decided to try and stay as near the front as possible. The fates were with me. Just inside, at a wide section with no railings, the guide pointed out a bat, like a little brown golf-ball attached to the roof by a hairy stalk. The children surged forward with "Oohs" and "Aahs" and whatever "Yuk" is in Hungarian, while I slipped furtively behind them to the head of the queue. After that it was easy to saunter along at a leisurely pace until the mood was firmly set for the group.

Aggtelek is at one end of an enormous cave-system, that stretches for twenty-two kilometers underground before popping up at several entrances in Slovakia. This end is well organised as a show cave, with the best goodies saved for the end.

At first all was fairly ordinary, except for the density of tiny, needle-like stalactites decorating the roof. The colours embedded in the limestone varied fom dark grey through ochre to an occasional striking rust-red - often within the same formation, producing an original technicolour effect.

At about half-way the passage flowed into a vast, echoing cavern. With sharp-pointed stalactites hanging thickly from the ceiling, it looked like a Gothic cathedral turned inside-out. At the wider end it was jarringly fitted out with a stage and several hundred red plastic chairs. Decently hidden behind a group of stalagmites lurked a couple of Portaloos. (Who, I wondered, empties them; and how much are they paid to lug buckets of turds through half a mile of cramped passages to the open air?)

We were invited to sit down, and treated to a brief concert played on a synthesiser and relayed through hidden speakers to thunder around the cavern, while the guide did dramatic things with the lights. It was certainly impressive; a pity that all I could think of was to fear that the vibration might loosen the stalactites, looming overhead like a multiple Sword of Damocles. Various holes gaped between them. Come to think of it, considering the crocodile-teeth formations, the other strange excrescences dangling from the ceiling, the arched shape of the roof and the artificially raised bed of the auditorium, we could have been sitting on the tongue of a gigantic stone mouth. It would hardly have been surprising if the music had transformed itself into stomach rumbles, and we had all disappeared with a slurp.

Towards the end of the tour were some truly amazing chambers of limestone pillars and curtains, all in the same psychedelic colouring as before. And suddenly the open air received us, and we were making our way back to the entrance over a hillside covered with snowdrops and cowslips flowering together. I stopped to investigate a rustle in the bushes, and surprised a tiny slow-worm happily carrying home the obscene shrivelled body of a baby bird. One man's meat...

CHAPTER X: PARADISE REGAINED

We seemed to tread air rather than crusted snow; we were

light of foot; we walked like demigods in joyous serenity.

At last we... went down like fallen angels, with an ever-mounting

reluctance, from a spiritual paradise...

(W.H. Murray)

The good news was that the Slovak border was only a couple of hundred yards up the road from Aggtelek. The bad, that it was restricted, for Hungarian and Slovak nationals only. With one glance at my passport, the guard pronounced sentence of a forty-mile detour west.

A welcome general store in the middle of nowhere gave me the chance to unload my remaining Hungarian currency. The bubbly lady behind the counter quickly grasped my drift, adding extra bananas to the scales to fit my pile of notes in front of her, and finishing with a chocolate bar as a makeweight, which suited me nicely.

A mile further on, the border guard didn't believe that I hadn't so much as a single forint left. He looked me up and down suspiciously, as if planning a strip-search; then thought better of it and waved me irritably through.

Bound for Dobšiná and its ice-cave, I took minor roads up a pleasant valley, winding between steep hills forested with birch and fir. Throughout Slovakia, the roads are commonly planted with flowering trees. Here, it was wild cherry; later, double flowered, heavily perfumed garden cherries threw drifts of scent through the windows.

At Dobšiná, I learned that the ice-cave was further on, a mile's walk from the road and shut anyway. Maybe it wasn't such a good idea. Instead I took a short detour down to Dedinky, where a reservoir fills a wide, bowl-shaped hollow. The little village on its shore is a holiday centre, attracting visitors for walking and water sports in summer, and ski-ing in winter. Ski-ing? It can't be more than a couple of thousand feet above sea level. But sure enough, on some of the slopes were drag lifts, and here and there some tiny, rather pretentious avalanche barriers leaned out over modest hillsides.

The van pulled resolutely up the long, precipitous hill back to the main road. I stopped for the afternoon at a marvellous spot with views for miles, to lie on the grass eating a late lunch. Overhead was a buzzard that thought it was a lapwing, enjoying the warm updraughts with a display of lazy aerobatics. Unfortunately here the last canister of camping gas spluttered and died, leaving me with "hot" chocolate that demanded a spot of positive thinking.

The morning shift had been a long one. I was running late when I turned on to a minor road, crossed the River Hnilec and began the long pull uphill over the top of the mountainous area called the Slovenský Raj (pronounced "Rye"), or Slovak Paradise. The best of the day's light was already passing, and the surroundings didn't immediately suggest heaven, except for a hint in their altitude.

Crossing the tops meant driving back into winter. The beech twigs were still naked and snow lay in the corners and gullies. Most of the hills were heavily forested. Halfway up the long, winding climb, the trees drew back briefly to give a grand, though rather desolate view back down a long valley and up to the saddle on the other side. I didn't pass a single car throughout, and had the feeling that none had been up here for weeks. A vague sense of depression hovered round me. Its immediate cause remained elusive, until I pinned it down to the prospect of bed with no hot cup of tea.

At the end of a long downhill run, civilisation returned with small settlements and the occasional waymarker. I came out of the trees and turned east, looking constantly for Podlesok campsite to appear on the right. It was some distance before I casually glanced left; and then nearly drove off the road. I had to stop, get out of the van and gaze my fill.

In the hazy distance was a mountain ridge, far off but towering, strangely insubstantial in the mist: the High Tatras. They rose suddenly out of the plain with no foothills to lead the eye in gently, like the Skye Cuillin out of the Minches. In fact everything about them - the shape, the notched outline, the continuity of the ridge - was hauntingly reminiscent of Skye. Even the individual peaks bore uncanny resemblance; involuntarily I picked out what might have been the twin tops of Alasdair and Thearlaich, the rounded hump of Sgurr Dearg, the classic V of Gillean and the triple cleft peak of Bidean Druim na Rabh. Until five years ago, such mountains had figured importantly in my life. Past memories seethed; my pulse quickened in anticipation of the following day, when I hoped to recapture some fleeting whiff of the good old days.

At the campsite, a friendly red-haired man gave me a hearty welcome. Yes, of course I could stay, although he was only just opening and no-one else had arrived yet. He gave me a map, showed me the best routes into the hills and even - Good Samaritan - filled my thermos. To my repeated expressions of thanks and delight he queried, "*Prima*?! Terrific?!" over and over, his red quirky eyebrow shooting up into his hairline. "Yes, prima!" I got the message at last, and he beamed with satisfaction.

The showers weren't heated yet, so my new friend took down a key and led me to a row of neat, painted chalets that edged the site. With the genial air of an expansive host he gave me the run of one. There I stood for indulgent long minutes, mouth open, under a blessed stream of warm water, until I was slaked, inside and out. Then it was the turn of my clothes.

Afterwards, my spot chosen at leisure from a good three acres, all deserted, I enjoyed my first hot drink for several hours, or a lifetime; slung a line of knickers between the van and a fence post; and went to bed. Early: I had plans for the next day.

*

The Slovenský Raj covers 125 square miles of limestone plateau, deeply scored by a dozen gorges. Through these, streams alternately meander along rock-strewn beds alive with wild flowers, or tumble merrily through crevices and over waterfalls on their way to join either the Hnilec River southwards, or the larger Hornad which separates the uplands from the Hornadská Plain to the north. The forested slopes offer pleasant walking, but the real excitement of the Raj lies in the ravines, whose otherwise impassable crags and waterfalls are made accessible to walkers by a series of fixed iron ladders, steps and bridges.

My route was the Sucha Bela, running due south from the campsite into the heart of the plateau. The name means White Valley, though it was colour coded green on map and waymarkers. I didn't intend to follow it far: just to the first ladder system, and possibly up and a little way beyond if my legs were behaving.

The track followed the stream. I stayed more or less in it, trading the discomfort of wet feet against the greater effort of the undulating path alongside. It was full of the debris of winter: tree trunks snapped off and splintered like matchwood, with here and there a wooden pallet washed down from the upper reaches.

The banks, now receding, now closing in tightly, were smothered in cowslips, blue anemones and violas, under thick woods of fir and beech. The area is famed for its wildlife - there are said to be lynx and otters here, and nearly two thousand species of butterfly have been recorded - but the sound of the running water obscured all other noises but my own, and the locals obviously heard me well before I saw them. The only exception was a pair of spotted woodpeckers high in the canopy of leaves.

It felt like miles to the first artificial climb. Slowly the cliffs drew in, rising sheer overhead to two hundred feet or more. At last I turned a corner and saw, above an old, grubby snow-bank, a twenty-foot ladder beside a sheer waterfall. At its top, grill-like steps and a rusty chain disappeared encouragingly round a blind corner into a cleft. A short rest, and I was ready to climb.

There was no scope for letting the legs wobble, so I didn't. If this was Paradise, I would pass on the harp, but could certainly use a pair of wings.

I was thankful when I reached the top and, turning the corner, was able to sit in the cleft for a while. Above and below the water thundered down. The rocks glistened with spray. But for the thin light slithering down into the crack, I might have been several hundred feet under the Mendips, rather than above the Slovakian Plain.

A bridge and a couple of shorter ladders led on out of the cleft. And suddenly I was at the top and out in the sunlight, lying on my back and gasping like a beached fish; and intensely pleased with life.

It was a pleasant spot. I idled over my lunch, listening to the slap and gurgle of the stream and suppressing as long as possible the inevitable, insidious thought, "Wouldn't it be nice to go a bit further and take a look at the next section...?" - but keeping back a sandwich or two without deliberate intention. Subconsciously, the question was already asked, and answered.

For a bit the going was easy. Then once again the rock walls narrowed, and the temperature dropped like a stone as the way entered a ravine. Its sides were sandpapered to smoothness by thousands of years of ice and water, and here and there were windows in projecting buttresses. Wooden walkways kept my feet dry as I insinuated myself between the close walls. High above, tongues of ice lolled out of cavernous holes in the rock-face; while down below were odd pockets of warm air, deposited unexpectedly by some whimsical current.

A little further, and I arrived at the final series of ladders, less dramatic this time. Deliberately not stopping to think, I went for the top, and before long was once again flat out and recharging. Now it was high time to declare the day a success, and head for home. But by now my boats were thoroughly burned.

The Sucha Bela, like the other gorges in the Slovenský Raj, is designated a one-way path - a strange concept, until you try to imagine how two parties might cross in the middle of a hundred-foot series of airy, hairy ladders, "...gin a body meet a body, comin' thro' the Raj!"

Today, this wasn't a problem. I had the area to myself, and there could be no fear of a traffic jam. But by now my legs were seriously knackered. Climbing down in any circumstances is more dodgy than climbing up; with my knees shaking and little co-ordination left, there was a distinct risk of going down faster than intended, and with no-one for miles to scrape up the bits.

This was good news; after all I could find lots of reasons for going on, not all of them spurious. Come to think of it - the first time I honestly had - to return the way I had come was a pointless effort which had never been a serious option. It was top or bust.

The path left the main stream, and continued up a parallel gully. This was the home stretch, but the hardest walking - gently but relentlessly uphill. I began to set myself so many steps between rests, feeling like Fanny Robin on Casterbridge Highway; and made it at last.

They really meant the one-way bit. At this end was a stern "No Entry" sign, as if plucked from a city street. Close by, and more friendly, was a spring, parent of the Sucha Bela stream, lovingly boxed into a little gabled hut. I drank gratefully and greedily, mindful of the hours still ahead.

It had taken four hours to do the two miles so far. The route down, however, was a forestry track, more direct and steadily downhill.

Disappointingly, here at the meeting of the ways there were no good views. The meadow nearby was a mass of late crocuses, but tall trees enclosed it. Worse, the picnic table and signpost were surrounded by horrific piles of last year's cans, marinading gently in goodness knew what unidentifiable grot. At least there was nothing wrong with the seat. Unfortunately my food was finished, and I sat and fantasised about bacon sandwiches followed by slabs of chocolate until I could bear it no longer, and got wearily to my feet.

My new path was coded yellow; "Follow the yellow brick road" said my brain over and over, like an irritating child, trying to will my feet to march to the rhythm. Now and again the trees thinned briefly to allow glimpses to the north. Neat red-roofed settlements appeared and disappeared, seeming to shift and dodge like a mirage between one sighting and the next, until I wasn't sure whether I had seen four villages, or one village four times. Above the plain, levitating in the haze, stood the ridges of the High Tatras.

There was a sudden movement in the bushes, and I found a red squirrel giving me the once-over. Two could play at that game. I stalked him for a photograph, but he shot higher and away, clicking abuse while twitching his tail to time, like a conductor's baton. Long after he had vanished across a bridge of branches, I could follow his path by the torrent of invective streaming back through the leaves.

Towards the end of the downward stretch I met a party of three middle-aged people. They had heard of the scenic waterfall routes and wanted to try them. Could I tell them the way? I showed them the map, but advised them against trying. They weren't dressed for it; their "sensible" shoes wouldn't have given a grip on the ladders, and one of the women wore a tight skirt.

It gave me a rare sense of elation, to have managed something that these fit and "normal" people couldn't do. The feeling gave me a second wind for the last quarter-mile. At last I heard a skylark through the trees, which meant that level, open ground wasn't far off. A moment later I turned a corner to the infinitely welcome sight of the van a hundred yards away. Minutes later I was horizontal, thankfully airing my sweaty feet and celebrating with the chocolate I'd been dreaming of two hours earlier.

*

My red-haired friend was off shift. I said my goodbyes to a stranger, and set off in search of a town to paint red. Ten miles up the road was the perfect destination.

The solid mediaeval walls of Levoča, now a sleepy little town long past its heyday, bear witness to a grander past, including four centuries as a rich provincial capital. The main road passes under an imposing gatehouse, immediately beyond which lies the town square. Regiments of heavily pollarded, knobbly trees give a French "feel" to the place, and I was reminded of the little Camargue town of Aigues Mortes.

The focal point of the square is at the far end, where two churches, one Catholic and the other Protestant, confront each other across the neutral face of the Rathaus. They are said to be packed with art treasures. Unfortunately they wouldn't be open until May - now only two days away, but still too late.

Not all of Levoča was chocolate box material. Many of the other buildings were in a poor state of repair, and several had windows plugged with concrete blocks. Gangs of the local youth mooched around the streets with boredom written all over them; while from a disco down the road came the noise of somebody inappropriately and very loudly playing "Last Christmas I gave you my heart." Surrounded by the past, both recent and remote, the teenagers here must be pretty frustrated. No wonder so many windows were bricked up.

Tonight, however, I would have been pleased with a piece of Brixton or Milton Keynes. Intoxicated by my first "proper" walk for five years, I thrilled to the obvious charms of the place. A wander through the grid of side roads brought me to the far wall, beyond which a bank smothered in cowslips led down to allotments at the bottom. I walked along on top of the wall and past a crumbling watchtower, and came back to the main gatehouse.

Nearby was a likely-looking restaurant. It exceeded all hopes, with a wonderful and absurdly cheap meal. Afterwards I sat outside in the little courtyard under a darkening sky, indulging in endless cups of tea until the last patron had gone home, and the waitress was glancing at me covertly, wondering when she would be able to do the same.

So I paid my bill, left a large tip and removed myself to a park bench in the square. This wasn't the occasion for an early night. The stars were brilliant, while the soaring half-moon seemed a potent symbol of my own state: halfway there and still gaining.

*

I would gladly have spent the night there, on my park bench under the stars. Instead I drove east, up an endless hill, and stopped at a spot looking down on the lights of Levoča a few miles away. Eating a final supper - shameless greed! - I went to bed, anticipating the dreamless sleep of content. But the night wasn't over yet.

Past midnight I was woken by light, hustle, shouting; and a peremptory tattoo on the van door. Surrounding the van were four military police toting sub-machine guns and radiating hostility. Someone should have told them the Cold War was over. Not me; even if I could speak Slovak, I wasn't going to get a word in edgeways, against a diatribe of which the only comprehensible word was "Passport".

I opened the window a crack and handed it over. It was rudely snatched and inspected. Almost throwing it back at me, the leader picked up my bag of perishable food, left outside for coolness, and shook it angrily by the window; and with this mystifying gesture they departed as suddenly as they had come.

XI: NIGHT ON THE BARE MOUNTAIN

Pitiless giants with rock-bound crest,

Mystical wells for the midnight rest,

Ice-crowned castles and halls...

(Geoffrey Winthrop Young)

It was mainly in search of heat that I went to Poprad; heat in the form of more gas, more fuses for the long-defunct kettle, or preferably both. This was just as well, as it wasn't a town to be visited for purely aesthetic reasons.

Here, for the first time in my experience, was small-time urbanised Slovakia, a world away from the Slovensky Raj or even Levoča. The industrial outskirts, far from self-effacing, were almost aggressively functional and rather grubby. The town centre, itself once a small village with a pretty church, was depressingly encircled by tower blocks which did their best - although without entirely succeeding - to blot out the grand backdrop of the Tatras.

I combed the streets without success, and was about to give up when a small, unobtrusive sports shop delivered the goods - one of them, anyway - in unfamiliar bright yellow cylinders. But the shape of the cartridge wasn't quite a perfect fit, and for nailbiting minutes the stove grimly rejected all efforts to marry the two.

The attendant summoned reinforcements. Along came the manager, who grappled with the cylinder for some minutes until it suddenly popped into place. Someone produced matches, while I fidgeted in suspense; then the stove lit up with a triumphant Whoosh! Don't kiss the manager, I thought; remember you've nearly been arrested once already. So I stammered my thanks and staggered out loaded with five cylinders, to the silent amusement of the staff. Poprad was suddenly beautiful.

Outside the town, the mountains, now only a couple of miles distant, reared to a great height. The lie of the land means that here, from the south, the escarpment is very sudden; whereas on the Polish side of the border (which runs along the topmost ridge) it is much gentler.

The winter sports resorts of Starý Smokovec and Tatranská Lomnica were in sleepy limbo, with only a handful of skiers left and the summer walking season not yet begun. I took the cable car up Lomnický Štít, the second highest peak in the Tatras, from which the village below takes its name.

In the car were four or five damp, sweaty skiers, going up for the last few runs of the afternoon. The encrusted snow on their legs and boots melted steadily in the late April warmth, dripping over my feet and steaming up the windows, so that I could barely see the approaching peaks.

The man at the halfway station said that the last stretch to the top was closed for lack of demand. Even here, though, the scenery was spectacular, the views breathtaking. It was electrifying to be in real mountains again. The air at this altitude sparkled like champagne. I swallowed great lungfuls, enough to last me all the way home; then scrunched around in the snow, watching the few remaining dedicated skiers scratching down tired moguls. At last I retreated from the cold into the cafe, to sit writing my diary over a cup of tea. All the way back down I was planning my return visit, just as soon as I could strap on a pair of skis again.

*

It was towards evening when I took to the road again. Well before I reached the border the sun had already set, throwing a fiery pink light behind the mountains. I was in two minds whether to stop or go on. But there was no suitable parking place immediately obvious. Anyway I had an ·idiotic compulsion to stick to my timetable, which demanded that I should be in Poland that night.

Moreover I fancied the idea of staying in the hostel by Morskie Oko, the famously beautiful lake high in the mountains. Its name means "eye of the sea", for the story has it that an underground stream links the lake to the distant Baltic. There wouldn't be much of a view there tonight, but the thought of waking up to it tomorrow was irresistible.

The border formalities were the lengthiest yet. It was quite dark by the time I had queued to change money behind a mournful looking Pole with a Lech Wałęsa moustache and a week's stubble. It didn't help that I then drove five miles in the wrong direction.

Getting it right at last, I found myself on a rough road pulling sharply uphill for six miles. On the way I passed five climbers footslogging it up with enormous rucksacks, ice axes dangling behind. Their spokesman, a young Pole who spoke fluent English (I learnt it in school, he said self-deprecatingly) explained that they planned to climb Rysy, the highest peak on the Polish side.

I couldn't fit them all in, but offered to give their rucksacks a lift. Gratefully they slung them in the back, and continued with new life in their steps. Meanwhile the poor little van, its springs groaning, was barely able to leave them behind. I later tried to lift one of the rucksacks, but couldn't. I reckoned each weighed upward of fifty pounds. Hard men!

Disappointment was waiting at the top. Yes, there was room at the hostel, said the warden. It wasn't me but the van that was the problem. Not only might I not park there; I shouldn't have driven up at all. Didn't I know that this was the Tatra National Park?

I didn't, and grovelled duly; adding by way of excuse that there was no alternative, as I couldn't walk up. Tough, he said. Cars simply weren't allowed, and the offending vehicle must be taken away forthwith. But he did send one of his staff to unload the rucksacks, and I was grateful for the small mercy.

Before leaving, I felt entitled to walk down to the lake. Immediately, all the evening's frustrations vanished. The moon, making up in height what it still lacked in fullness, threw brilliant light over Rysy. Standing a little out on the ice, I could pick out every detail of the connecting ridges, etched in white and the deepest blue.

It was better than daylight, and honour was more than satisfied. And had I not come like a thief in the night, Officialdom would certainly have stopped me at the bottom of the road, and Morskie Oko would have remained just an entry in the guide book.

*

By the time I found somewhere to pull off the Zakopane road and stop, it was gone ten and I was all in. The threat of worse, however, was approaching.

As well as the more or less constant physical exhaustion, my brain was as mushy as if I were heavily drunk. I was doing all sorts of silly things: setting off on the wrong side of the road three times in the last two days, continually bashing my head on the van ceiling and generally getting terribly muddled over trivialities. Some very promising headaches had been winding themselves up, my mouth was full of ulcers and an ominous sore throat was brewing.

By next morning my worst fears were confirmed. The throat had gone from whinging to raging, with cold sweats, feverishness and a lovely concoction of aches and pains. It was a great start to a new country.

This wasn't something I had "caught", but rather a familiar case of The Beast Bites Back; what I have come to refer to as "false 'flu". For many people with ME, it seems that in a really bad patch the virus semi-dormant in the system takes advantage and runs riot, causing anything from brief violent fever to a longer, milder attack like 'flu. Either way, on top of the underlying illness, hopelessly incapacitating. I knew from experience that, if I was eventually to get back on the road with the minimum of time lost, the only course was to give in at once and lie up.

At least the weather was on my side. With the sudden whim of mountain regions, banks of cloud built up, and soon a steady drizzle began to fall. There was no incentive to move. Also, a rest day was due; and a look at the map showed that by simply omitting a dog-leg west of Warsaw I could cancel a couple more days without getting badly behind.

Meanwhile, I had the new gas to try out, an infinite supply of teabags and the excuse of a sore throat to lubricate... and a new Dick Francis in the book-box. Things could have been worse.

*

Zakopane has been Poland's favourite mountain resort for a century or more. The numbers of climbers, walkers and skiers who collect here throughout the year have inevitably left their mark, and the town struggles to maintain its integrity against an ever-increasing sprawl of suburbs. But at heart, and in its centre, it remains a mainly unspoilt, attractive Alpine village.

Its fine old chalet-style houses would look equally at home in Chamonix or Grindlewald, although the newer buildings on the outskirts are badly disfigured by what looks like stainless steel roofing. But the outstanding feature of the universal wooden architecture must surely be the little church on the Bystre road out of the centre.

Its whimsical, almost pagoda-like appearance tempted me in for a closer look. Inside, literally everything was of wood: the altar, the pulpit, even the chandelier with its six lights. In one corner stood a tiny harmonium, boxed in so as to seem at first glance to be a confessional.

Outside, the streets hummed with tiny Fiat "Polska" bubble cars, 650cc and definitely not the sort to get stuck behind on a hill. (Like, to be truthful, 970cc vans.) Ranks of them were parked by a wide grassy field on the road into town, so that I simply had to stop and see what was going on.

Above a former ski-slope, now new grass with only a few icy patches left over, the National Paragliding Championships were in progress. Contestants rode the chairlift up the wide strip cleared through the forest, and disappeared over the brow of the hill, to appear half an hour later airborne, drifting down on a flimsy scrap of material to the spectators waiting below.

I joined the idling Saturday afternoon crowd to laze on the grass in the sunshine, watching a succession of tiny floating specks turn slowly into multi-coloured, giant butterflies, and attempt to land on a mattress painted with a bullseye. Even for the non-urgently competitive, there was a strong incentive to get it right. Just beyond the landing area was a tangle of spiky-looking elders, while all around the field had been recently and generously muck-spread.

The haphazard pattern of streets around the new development confused me, and it was on a sort of decreasing circle that I finally spiralled my way into the centre of town. First things first; for once I would patronise the campsite here, as I was now urgently in need of hot water and a good scrub. I found it to the south-east, by a large meadow leading up towards the hills in general, and in particular to two huge, terrifying looking ski-jumps built for past Winter Olympics.

The hot water, however, was a fantasy. This wasn't a serious contender for Poland's cleanest site. Various fake loo signs led into rubbish sheds, testing the perseverance of the punter; the real thing stank like an oriental squatter. The shower had two taps, Cold and Very Cold, while coming out of it cleaner than I went in presented quite a challenge, even in my squalid state.

*

Zakopane's entrepreneurial class had no hang-ups about Sunday trading. The smarter shops were closed to all except window shoppers, but open stalls sprouted like mushrooms along the main streets in the centre.

Bargain of the week were the hand-knitted woollen sweaters, piled high on booths manned - if I may put it that way - by wrinkled old ladies from the surrounding villages who probably knocked them out at the rate of three or four a week. The colours were natural, in cream, white and all imaginable shades of grey, and the workmanship impeccable. I have seen such jumpers selling for fifty or sixty pounds in the craft shops of Western Scotland or the Hebrides. Here, they were 120,000 zlotys, just a fiver. I bought several as gifts.

The other principal raw material was, of course, wood. I searched in vain for cuckoo clocks or musical boxes for nephews and nieces, remembering the fun such presents had given me years ago; but the goods here were less sophisticated, and I settled for wooden pictures, wooden farms, wooden weathercocks.

It was a good job the banks were closed, or I would have cleaned out the town. Private money-changers popped up at every corner - in street booths, or huddling over a small counter in a shop doorway - but they refused travellers' cheques, and my cash supply was limited, consisting mainly of dollars which I was hoarding for the Baltic states. Even so, I had to repack the van before I could drive on.

*

To the west of the town the Chocholowska valley runs south into the heart of the High Tatras to its source in a corrie hard by the Slovak border. It is a famous beauty spot, and I hoped to explore it a little way in the van. So far it hadn't been possible to see as much of the mountains at close range as I had hoped, and anyway the name sounded right up my street.

Frustration again. Just as things began to look promising, the edge of the National Park loomed up, the road was closed to cars and it was feet or nothing.

Even so far downstream, though, the valley deserved its reputation. I spent the afternoon sitting in a meadow among cowslips and giant roseroot, and drinking copious tea made with water straight off the mountains; about as near as I ever came to really tasting them.

The fields around - not so much fields as spaces between the tracts of forest - were purple with wild crocuses. The cattle and sheep were newly out to pasture, still milling from habit round the wooden barns. Again, the atmosphere was entirely Alpine. Perhaps mountains the world over stamp their own style on surrounding communities in a way quite independent of nation or culture.

But these mountains, for me, remained remote, almost untouchable. They had suffered me to approach twice, briefly, at Lomnický Štít and again at Morskie Oko; but for the most part I had merely crawled round the edges like an ant, snubbed and excluded.

The fact is, of course, that it is only possible to "feel" the High Tatras, like all such places, through the soles of your feet. This meant that they were as far removed from me as the moon. I simply couldn't get at them on wheels.

Moreover, since the heady experience of the Slovenský Raj, my expectations had soared; while the savage backlash of that over-indulgence meant that my body's capacity had done just the opposite. The spirit had never been so willing, nor the flesh so weak - not simultaneously, anyway.

I felt at once unsatisfied and reluctant to leave, yet desperate to get away; the sum total being profound depression. But cloud was rolling in over the high peaks, while away to the north I could see the sun shining; and the hours were ticking away. As soon as the wheels hit the onward road my black mood lifted, and within a few miles I was singing my heart out and, mentally at least, back on top of the world.

Instead of heading due north for Kraków I took the scenic route, passing through more of yesterday's Alpine meadows to follow the Chocholowska

Valley to Chocholow village. Here, you get the full impact of the prevailing wooden architecture: not self-consciously pretty, to impress the tourists as in Zakopane, but real, down-to-earth, functional, as it must have been originally conceived. Yet these houses were beautiful, too, with exquisite carving along the verandahs, or even on a barn door.

The gentle, rolling countryside held one or two more such unspoiled villages, though none rivalled the unsophisticated elegance of Chocholow. Before I rejoined the main road again at Nowy Targ, the last of the wooden cottages was behind me, and brick and concrete were once again in charge.

CHAPTER XII: HERE BE DRAGONS

This is the weather the cuckoo likes,

And so do I;

When showers betumble the chestnut spikes,

And nestlings fly.

(Thomas Hardy)

It was downhill all the way to Kraków. And in the course of an afternoon I passed, once again and this time for good, into full spring.

Zakopane's trees were still, in early May, quite bare, the pasture grey with recent thaw. Within thirty miles or so, the buds were splitting to show the first green, and I was back among cherry and pear blossom.

I stopped for the afternoon in a meadow where the birch leaves were halfway open and the grass already thick and glossy. Wild flowers grew all around; and a bee crawled over my pillow, leaving a rambling yellow trail of pollen before I shooed her out of the door.

Afterwards, for fully half an hour the road followed the course of a river, along whose banks families strolled at evening leisure. Near the lower end there was apple blossom to join the pear, and from here on to the very eastern edge of Poland the road was bordered with orchards in riotous spring bloom.

These roads were the best since leaving western Germany: clean-cut, with a good surface, clearly marked with fresh paint, and a wide hard shoulder. The traffic signs, in luminous yellow, red and black, couldn't be missed. They also looked brand-new. The level crossing signs, with their silhouette of a stream train, were rather out of place.

The hard shoulder was constantly used by slower vehicles to allow faster ones to pass - in both directions. I quickly learned to watch the traffic like a hawk, so as to be ready to move over before an overtaking car approaching head-on, or to allow the one behind to pass. The little Fiats drove constantly half-straddled over the edge, with deferential humility.

The last miles into Kraków passed in a haze of blossom, and on its streets flowered rowan, chestnut and even lilac. The transition from March to May had been accomplished in a few hours.

*

I had originally intended to avoid Kraków altogether. It may have been for centuries the seat of the Polish kings and sometime capital of empires; yet in living memory it has become tainted by one of the greatest evils in the history of man, through its association with the Nazi death camp of Auschwitz-Birkenau.

It would have been a shame, though, to bypass what is generally considered to be historically, architecturally and culturally one of Europe's leading cities. And my first sight of its streets, beautiful in their spring clothes, did much to alter my blinkered preconceptions.

Here at last the original plan worked: namely, to arrive in a city in the quiet of evening and drive around, getting my bearings, seeing as much as possible from the van and working out where best to park and explore on foot. In an astonishing absence of traffic I meandered around the streets of Kazimierz, for nearly five centuries the old Jewish Quarter and cultural vortex of Polish Jewry.

Kraków was largely undamaged in the second War, and Kazimierz is full of signs of its past. I found a number of synagogues, two of them once more in use. Behind a high wall, the old Jewish Cemetery was filled with spring flowers. The suburb was never exclusively Jewish, and there were churches, too; the rather gloomy Corpus Christi, hemmed in by tall, dark buildings, and St. Catherine's to the west, bright and welcoming within its spacious garden.

It was still light, and a morbid impulse took me across the river to the site of the wartime Jewish ghetto. A small part of its wall still stands, with a memorial inscription. Here, you couldn't help thinking of the story of Otto Schindler; for it was just here that the German industrialist wrought his miracles, saving hundreds from the gas chambers by insisting on the need for cheap Jewish labour in his factory.

Nothing besides the wall remains. The area is now innocently covered with housing, shops and moderately busy streets. It is oppressive only by association. Nevertheless I was glad to pay my respects and hurry back across the river to monuments from kinder centuries.

Back in the centre, I scouted after likely parking places for the next day, then took advantage of the evening quiet to leave the van and wander into the Rynek Główny, or town square. For once the timing was right. I arrived at eight, just as the trumpeter sounded the hour from the spire of the Mariacki church.

The daylight was almost gone, and I was tired: no point in staying, as there

108

would be time enough to look around properly tomorrow. But it seemed too early for bed, so I took the van for a final aimless bumble round the streets. Too aimless; for I bumbled right through the pedestrianised area and into the Rynek, and had to make a rapid about turn and retreat. Definitely bedtime; and a quiet spot between the river and Wawel Hill fitted the bill perfectly.

*

I had the latest in a series of late starts, but it was worth waiting, as I got up at last in reasonable shape. Urban camping brought a return to the bucket. To my embarrassment I drove off leaving it indiscreetly in the middle of the street. As I reversed to pick it up, I felt all eyes swivel my way.

My luck was in, for I found the perfect parking place just at the foot of Wawel Hill. At once a waiting crowd caught my attention from a small square across the road. I joined them to stand expectantly for half an hour. Just as I was about to give it up and leave, along came a troop of middle-aged Boy Scouts, self-consciously wearing hairy legs under their shorts. They took up positions around the open space, to be followed by a military band, and finally by an assortment of uniformed and be-medalled characters.

These represented various military and civil bodies, some of whose outfits were spectacular. The final group - green hats with a feather, knee-length breeches and green woollen capes tossed casually over one shoulder - might have been extras off the set of The Prisoner of Zenda. They took their turn with the others, advancing in threes to lay wreaths at a plain wooden cross in the square. Today, it turned out, was Poland's Constitution Day, and for the rest of the day I kept bumping into various Bank Holiday fun and games.

There were no friendly buses or trams this time to take me up Wawel Hill. It is Kraków's Citadel, bearing as usual both Castle and Cathedral. Here for centuries was the royal residence and centre of government. Even after King Zygmunt III decided to move the capital to Warsaw four centuries ago, Polish kings continued to be crowned in Wawel Cathedral. Not long ago it again played a significant part in history when Karol Wojtyla was invested here as Archbishop of Kraków, on his way to the Vatican. The support of a Polish Pope did much to stiffen the resistance of Polish Catholicism to the Communist government, helping to hasten its demise.

Rather small for the spiritual centre of a large nation, the Cathedral has an atmosphere all the the more concentrated for having less space to fill. Down the sides, richly endowed chapels commemorate various King Kazimierzes and Ladislaws. At the head of the nave is a magnificent gilded shrine to St. Stanislaw, murdered a thousand years ago by a king whose ambitions he had opposed - a Polish Thomas á Becket.

Outside is a wide open space with low irregular walls. Now the framework for gardens, these walls are the foundations of a former township, cleared by last century's Austrian conqerors to make a parade ground. I stopped for a coke, and sat under pink chestnut candles soaking up the sun and the surroundings.

Legend tells how a cave under Wawel Hill was once the lair of a dragon, who, with the usual tastes of his kind, dined off beautiful maidens. After crunching his way through a number of unsuccessful knights errant, he was eventually slain by a lowly carpenter called Krak. The grateful king rewarded the man with precious gifts, and honoured him by giving his name to the city.

If there were ever caves under the Hill, they are long since destroyed or filled in. But the narrow alleys at its foot were dark enough to feel like underground passages. I came into daylight by the Church of Saints Peter and Paul. The twelve apostles, frowning and resolute in stone, guarded its approach. From behind them a lively congregation was spilling into the street, their conversation punctuated by loud notes from the organ voluntary.

A little way up the road, and I arrived once more in the open spaces of the Rynek. It was just one o'clock; time for the trumpeter to signal the hour from each face in turn of the Mariacki Church tower. Exactly so his thirteenth century predecessor signalled the arrival of the Tartar army, only to be cut off in mid-note by a Mongol arrow. He was the first of many, for the city was wasted by the Tartars. Among the casualties was the church itself, rased by the invaders. The current building is a mere stripling of six centuries old.

I hadn't finished with the Rynek, but now made my way through the leisurely Bank Holiday crowds, and past the ranks of flower sellers, towards the northern streets. Reaching the only remaining section of the old city walls, I came to the Floriańska Gate, a small portal surmounted by a great tower. Just beyond is the Barbakan, once part of a massive double defence but now isolated. The walls stretch back to towers on either side, and the local artists make good use of them to hang their paintings.

Back up Floriańska Street, I found the oldest hotel in Kraków. Its visitors' book includes Franz Liszt and Honoré de Balzac, but it is now known mainly as a casino. Over its doorway is the Latin inscription "Stet domus haec donec fluctus formicama os ebibet et totem testudo perambulet orbem" - "Let this house stand until an ant's mouth drinks the sea dry and a tortoise walks across the whole world". Obviously a powerful blessing: the house has lasted half a millennium, and looks good for a few more centuries yet.

The Rynek itself is Europe's largest mediaeval town square. Surrounded by churches and grandiose houses - many of them now cafés and restaurants - it is dominated by the massive stonework of the Sukiennice. Some hundred yards long, arched below and gargoyled above, Kraków's former cloth-market now houses an art gallery on the upper floor, while the lower is an arcade of market stalls. Outside, close by, is a solitary tower, its dark brick and stone gloomy against the pale honey of the Sukiennice. Perhaps it still mourns its other half, the town hall once joined to it, but pulled down nearly two centuries ago.

Passing under the double-arched doorway into the Sukiennice's market, I had to pause a moment while my eyes adjusted from the bright sunlight to the comparative gloom. As I began to see again, I found myself in a bazaar more in keeping with the souks of Damascus or Aleppo than a provincial European capital.

Both sides of the arcade were teeming with tiny stalls. Goods crammed the shelves, spilled over into the pathway, climbed up the walls and dangled from the roof. Each booth specialised in something different: lacework and embroidered peasant blouses; woollens, sheepskins and sweaters; woodwork ranging from the rudely carved toys like those I had bought in Zakopane up to beautifully crafted carvings and painted Russian matroshka dolls. Even this early in the year the crowds were thick, and elbow room at the counters was at a premium.

Once again I was strapped for cash. Constitution day had filled the streets but emptied and locked the banks, and more of my precious dollars went to the moneychangers. I bought matroshkas for my smaller friends and painted wooden boxes for their parents, and tried on one of the smocked blouses myself. One look in the mirror that the vendor held up to me, and I changed my mind. I hadn't used anything bigger than a driving mirror for a fortnight, and the face staring back at me was wrinkled and haggard with the aftermath of the Slovenský Raj. A black woollen shawl would have been more appropriate. I ripped off the pretty thing, made feeble excuses about the colour, and fled.

*

Clean out of zlotys, I had some worries about petrol, for Poland's filling stations didn't yet think much of plastic. Tonight the van's fuel would outlast my own, but first thing tomorrow I must find a bank taking travellers' cheques.

I stopped for the afternoon at a lake a few miles north of Kraków. It was obviously a favourite holiday afternoon spot, judging by the number of families idling or playing at its edge. Favourite, too, for the gulls which had somehow found their way over three hundred miles from the sea to colonise its central island. It wasn't long enough before I pressed on, anxious to get as much mileage under my belt as possible of the long haul up towards Warsaw, which was to be the longest continuous stretch of the whole trip.

The rolling hills flattened out to a central plain. It would have been tedious if it hadn't been so colourful. This was fruit-growing country, and I drove through a blur of pink, green, white and yellow - the last coming from the thick carpet of dandelions by the roadside.

The wayside shrines added their own splash of colour. Their low crosses were dressed for the holiday in a variety of styles; armfuls of flowers, coloured bunting and - once - twists of paper and cloth, a throwback to old pagan customs brought from Asia. I passed several churches under construction, a sign of the vigour with which the Catholic Church has thrived and grown since the Communists went.

Although this was a major road, there was only one sizeable town. The rest was rural. Horses and carts shared the road with motor traffic. As many horse-drawn ploughs as tractors worked the fields. Here and there an elderly lady sat by the roadside with a trailerload of apples for sale. She was often accompanied by the family cow, tethered and placidly grazing while huge lorries roared past only inches away.

But the modern world was there, too, with frequent radar speed traps. The speed limit on Polish roads is comparatively low; I would have been caught red-handed several times over, but for the warning of drivers coming the other way.

With an eye on the fuel gauge, I reckoned on Radom as the furthest town I could reach before changing money, and turned off the main road a little way south to find a suitable spot for the night. The area was fairly populous, and it was only after some searching that I pulled off the road under some trees and tried to get an early night.

No such luck. I was woken some time after midnight by a loud rapping on the van door. Outside were a couple of young policemen, rather officious, obviously bored with their night shift and looking for something to happen. I showed them my passport, made sure that I wasn't illegally parked, pleaded no Polish and thought I'd got rid of them.

Ten minutes later they were back, with a colleague even more officious. He embarked on a lengthy argument with me, uninhibited by total lack of mutual understanding, except for the word "dangerous", which he repeated boringly often and backed up by melodramatic theatre with a pistol. The fact that my "Bullshit" turned out to be also in his English vocabulary sent Anglo-Polish relations below freezing point. It was indicated that I was to accompany them, complete with van, to the Police Station.

I nearly answered, more out of bolshiness than anything else, that I had taken a sleeping pill and couldn't drive anywhere before morning. But I bit my tongue just in time. Although I had copies of my prescription with me just in case, the mention of drugs of any sort could only inflame the situation - especially given the language problem. I had envisaged many ways in which this trip might founder, but being banged up in a Polish nick for possession wasn't among them.

Hoping that my drug-dilated pupils wouldn't be spotted under the arc lights of the interrogation room, I climbed into the driving seat with a conspicuous ill-grace and followed carefully through a maze of country lanes, going very slowly and taking good care not to bounce off any trees. It would serve them right, I thought sourly, if my remaining thimbleful of petrol chose this moment to run out, and they had to tow me in.

Arriving was an anti-climax. They simply parked me in the garden and indicated, looking very pleased with their own chivalry, that I was to spend the night there. I'm sure they meant well, but couldn't help believing that entertainment, not altruism, was behind it.

*

Daylight showed me a back garden with a row of fat cabbages, which I'd watered the previous night under cover of darkness. There was a Land-Rover parked behind me, and signs of life from the Police Station. I kept the curtain pulled, so as not to let on that I was awake. I wasn't entirely sure they'd finished with me.

After some time two men emerged from the building and drove away in the Land-Rover. I waited a few minutes then did the same, trying not to look too furtive. Somehow I'd noted the turning to Radom through my mental fog the night before, and so got away smartly. The petrol held out, and soon the van was invisible among the increasing flow of traffic entering what was an averagely unattractive small industrial town.

To my dismay, even here the bank didn't take travellers' cheques. The precious pile of dollars shrank horribly. But at least I now had enough money in my pocket, and fuel in my tank, to reach Warsaw, which would surely deliver the goods.

The map showed a short cut across country to Zelazowa Wola, the birthplace of composer Frederic Chopin. I turned off the main road at Grójec bound for Mszczonów*, which sounded more like a noise made by Ivor the

* pronounced Msh-chonoff

Engine than a Polish town; and rapidly found myself on, first, cobbles, then a dirt track topped with a six-inch layer of dust. Driving on it was an acquired art. The trick, it seemed, was to take the centre of the road, straddling the biggest dust bank. If you left the wheel ruts the immediate skid felt more like driving a boat than a car.

Some short cut. It felt as if hours were added to the journey. Frustrated and hungry, I stopped at Żyrardów, another small industrial town, in search of bread - also unobtainable over the Bank Holiday - and found only chocolate, which was a bad move. A busy open market lured me in for a look, but it was rather sleazy, its goods just dismal rubbish. It nicely rounded off a rather irritating morning.

*

Some thirty miles west of Warsaw, Zelozowa Wola honours its famous son with a museum, souvenir shop and gardens. The first, in Chopin's own house, was frustratingly closed for repairs, draped with ladders and surrounded by lorries. The second and third were very much open. I bought postcards and a couple of cassettes - Polonaises, of course - from a friendly lady at the till, then enjoyed the park for an hour or so.

Part of it was formal, with a statue of the great man gazing reflectively over lawns and shrubberies. The most part, however, was rambling and gently wild, with just that degree of neglect which sets off perfectly the compulsive growth of early spring. Against a greenish lake plopping and crooning with hundreds of frogs stood the most perfect flowering crab apple.

I decided to treat myself to lunch at the restaurant opposite, rather than take the time and trouble to get out the stove. And a miserable treat it was. I splashed out on carp, at a price pretty excessive for Poland, and judging by the time it took to arrive, the chef must have trawled for it with a bent safety pin. It certainly hadn't spent the extra time in the oven, for when I dug in a knife it spurted blood, and I had to send it back for another try. It was another half-hour before it came back, after which time I'd eaten everything else in sight except the tablecloth, and my plate had been taken away. They gave me two forks to use, at which my patience ran out and I stormed into the kitchen to demand a knife.

When I got back, my mood did a sharp about-turn. By my table stood a little girl. I had dropped some post-cards in my tantrum; diffidently she collected them up and presented them to me. She had ash-blonde hair and blue eyes. Little over half a century ago, I thought, the Nazis scooped children like her off the streets and carried them away for inspection by "experts". They might be Aryan throwbacks, and must be placed with German foster-parents if their physical characteristics survived scrutiny. If not - if just one head measurement, say, came out wrong - the child was dumped in a concentration camp, and forgotten.

How many of this little girl's great-aunts and uncles, I wondered, had shared her looks, and suffered just that fate?

CHAPTER XIII: REINCARNATIONS

They were a powerful people, and great builders...

they thought their city would last for ever...

It was all down, down, down, gradually - ruin and

levelling and disappearance. Then it was all up, up,

up, gradually, as seeds grew to saplings, and

saplings to forest trees.

(Kenneth Grahame: The Wind in the Willows)

The Kampinoski Wilderness Area is Poland's largest National Park. Just as well, for lying as it does a few miles east of Warsaw, it is a favourite weekend and holiday playground for townspeople fed up with life in the metropolis. Low-lying and much of it marshy, it hugs the valley of the Vistula, Poland's longest river, which flows off the High Tatras through Kraków and Warsaw before emptying into the Baltic near Gdańsk.

The swamps, inland dunes and ancient woodland of the Kampinoski provide habitats for a catalogue of creatures, among them wild boar and beavers. The symbol of the Park is the elk, said to be here in large numbers.

Parking was potentially dicey, it being illegal to leave the road in a National Park. I'd had enough hassle when legally parked, and would rather have come face to face with a wild boar than another Polish policeman. Come to think of it, it would be rather nice to see a wild boar - from inside the van, of course. After some to-ing and fro-ing I found the perfect spot: deep in the forest, down a rough track graded as a road and therefore open to me, and in a sort of lay-by behind some trees. I prepared to turn off my interior light if any traffic came near, to avoid being visible after dark (something I stuck to from now on), but not a single vehicle passed.

Nor, sadly, did anything more interesting; although when I left the next day I followed the prints of a large deer which had walked up the exact centre of the track in the half-hour since the rain had stopped. On tip-toe, obviously.

It was time to muck out the van thoroughly, while fending off marauding mosquitoes with the numbers of Scottish midges and the teeth of English horseflies. I slept for ten hours and woke to heavy rain, which made it easy to stay put. When I finally set off, fifteen hours in bed and a tidy home had made a new woman of me.

*

The Zaborów Riding Centre occupies the grounds of a magnificent country house. Now rather decaying, its spacious yards and extensive accommodation give more than a hint of former wealth.

I had written in advance to try to arrange riding here, but hadn't got an answer. The Centre was obviously owned or managed by an uninterested figurehead, but in charge of its day-to-day running was a lady of whom the very reverse was true.

Barbara Spalińska was a little older than me, tall, her face framed with soft ginger curls. It was an arresting face: serene, gentle, kind. No difficult horse, you instinctively felt, would ever undermine her even temper; no slow pupil ever get the rough edge of her tongue. Yes, I could join a ride going out later that day, she said, and I could pay in dollars. She didn't know the exchange rate, but was prepared to take my word for it.

There were two hours to spare and Warsaw was only fifteen miles away. Ample time, I thought, to find the airport, more or less this side of the city, and change some money.

The traffic was heavy and I tried to navigate around the edge of the city. But road signs were a seriously endangered species in Warsaw. When by sheer luck I landed up on the airport road I hadn't seen a single one.

Coming back was even worse. I tried to stay even further out, which made no difference to the congestion. Perhaps everyone else had the same idea. Without seeing a single sign, I identified the arterial roads only by the position of the sun in relation to my very rudimentary map. It was more good luck than judgement which found me the right road; even then I had to travel ten miles on it by blind faith, until reaching a village with the wonderful and - more important - familiar name of Wigledy.

A quarter-hour late, I arrived red-faced and apologetic; but the other riders, all children, took some time to mount and it was thirty minutes before we rode out. No harm done.

The hour that followed was pleasant, if not the sheer heaven I had enjoyed with Equador. My mare Kora was lively and willing, with a comfortable stride. But the narrow woodland paths kept us in single file for much of the time. We followed a fat little girl with pigtails on a short-striding horse, forcing a running battle between myself and Kora as I tried to check her natural speed and avoid a collision; frustrating for her and tiring for me. At least my rear end had forgiven me for the earlier ill-treatment.

We crossed fields of young corn to reach the edge of the forest, and then plunged into a labyrinth of tracks which Barbara navigated with unerring certainty. The smells of spring enfolded us: the now-familiar scent of wild cherry, earth wet from the night's rain, damp young grass, dry old pine needles. Twice we saw deer, bounding across the ride in front of us to disappear among the trees, their white tails visible, like the Cheshire Cat's grin, long after the rest of them had vanished.

The mosquitoes, though, were the worst yet. Despite a long-sleeved shirt I was eaten alive, for they expertly found any exposed spot. Poor Kora carried dozens fixed to her, and before long my hand dripped with her own blood from slapping the bloated creatures.

When we could ride abreast, Barbara chatted in excellent English about her love for horses and her delight in her job. She had been riding for twenty years, the last four of which she had owned a horse, kept at the riding school.

Back at the stables we cemented the friendship over a cup of tea, and Barbara invited me home for supper. She loaded up her Fiat Polska with a troop of girls, horse-loving grooms and muckers-out who spent every available weekend and holiday working at the yard - much as I did at their age. We set off in convoy through a violent thunderstorm and back to the outskirts of Warsaw, stopping every so often to drop off one of the girls.

When we arrived, Barbara insisted that I get out the Wasp and secure the van. Theft, she said, was rife, and even within sight of the flat my things might not be safe. I was to remember her warning sooner than expected.

The block of flats, one of many identical such blocks, fitted the archetypal picture of life in a former Communist country: dingy inside and out, its stairwells smelling of urine. Inside Barbara's flat, cosy and comfortable, things couldn't have been more different. There was an exuberant welcome from her dog, and a quieter one from her mother and sister. We ate an Italo-Polish meal of borsch followed by spaghetti and washed down with lots of tea, while thunder and lightning crashed all around and the rain bucketed down.

Afterwards, Barbara told me something of life in the new Poland. The most immediate differences, she said, were the freedom to travel abroad and the disappearance of queueing as a way of life. I had already seen a little of the country's enormous agricultural resources. Now that its abundant food produce was no longer carted straight off to the Soviet Union, there was plenty for all. These days it was the Russians who went without, and the old joke, "What's two hundred feet long and eats cabbage? A Polish meat queue" belonged elsewhere.

I asked, inevitably, of Lech Wałęsa. Was it true that many Poles were becoming disenchanted with his Presidency? Yes, to some extent, she answered; although to many he retained hero status, and none would dispute either his courage or the amount he had achieved. But running a trade union, under however adverse circumstances, was a different thing altogether from running a country, and he was getting a very rough ride. But then, she added laughing, it was commonly said that for every one Pole you had two opinions. Poland was finding out that the democratic grass wasn't automatically greener.

(In fact later in the year distrust at the speed of reforms caused a major upset. To everyone's surprise, not least their own, the former Communists - now prudently renamed "Social Democrats" - were returned to power in the General Election. Freedom and food notwithstanding, the advent of a free market economy has led to a number of bullets to bite for the average Pole, higher rent and fuel prices, 15% unemployment and 30% inflation being only a few. Perhaps it wasn't so odd that the electorate plumped for the devil they knew.)

Politics can't hold the floor for long when two people with an interest in horses are in the same room. We soon dismissed the first for the more agreeable second. It was only much later, finally tired with talking, that we turned to the television.

Barbara's family had satellite TV, giving twenty or thirty channels in eight different languages. In my honour she found the BBC, on which the Foreign Secretary was pontificating on the latest diktat from Brussels. It seemed nothing much had changed since I'd gone away. We voted him out, and instead sat watching a video of International Dressage, oohing and aahing at levels of horsemanship which neither of us could even aspire to.

At last it was time for me to go. I took my leave and made for the centre of Warsaw, negotiating huge puddles left by the still rumbling thunderstorm. After a very quick recce of the centre I found a quiet spot among residential streets east of the river. I'd now been approximately vertical for a continuous eight hours, and needed a change in alignment.

It wasn't the best site yet. Urban camping meant a return to the hated bucket, and the noise and street lights kept me awake for hours. Just as well. I was still no more than drowsy when the van, sensitive to the least breath of wind, swayed almost imperceptibly. The trouble was, there was no wind. I pinned my ears back and lay very still. A moment later the passenger door squeaked quietly. Grabbing my siren alarm, I pulled back the curtain for a look. Nobody in sight. I must have imagined it.

I was about to go crossly back to bed, when I saw that the lock button, which I always neurotically checked at least three times every night, was open.

What made the back of my neck prickle was the speed. It couldn't have been opened any faster with its own key. The implications were horrific: even with the Wasp in place, such a thief could be in and out with my valuables before its eight-second timer went off.

I tied the front door handles to each other with string, and moved the van so that the back door - the only other with an external lock - was jammed up against the wall; another set of precautions which became part of the nightly ritual.

*

Warsaw's Rynek Starego Miasta, or Old Town Square, is a chocolate-box picture. Its decorative façades are painted in all the colours of the rainbow, often with human and animal figures, or abstract patterns, added for luck. It lacks the size, the impressive focal points, of the main squares of Kraków or Prague. The real force of its impact arises from its history.

Fifty years ago, not one brick was left standing on another, except as the haphazard constituent of a pile of rubble. The central Warsaw of today rose like a phoenix from the ashes of wholesale destruction wreaked by Nazi Germany.

Warsaw had already suffered heavy damage from bombing before the German occupation early in the war. In August 1944, as Hitler's Western Front began to crumble and Stalin's troops were pressing from the east, the Warsovians saw their opportunity. Almost the entire civilian population rose in a last-ditch attempt to throw off the Nazis and win freedom. But the Uprising failed. As the Poles dashed themselves to pieces against the Wehrmacht, the Soviet Army stood apart, cynically watching and waiting.

In reprisal the city, much of it already no more than a ghost town of bombed-out shells, was systematically rased to the ground - an act of malice on a scale difficult to grasp. Hitler, his own destruction only months away, gloated that the city of Warsaw was now no more than a name on the map of Europe.

But he reckoned without the tenacity and sheer guts of his victims. Immediately after the war ended, the people of Warsaw - now reduced, by some estimates, to one-third of their pre-war numbers by massacre or deportation - set themselves the task of rebuilding their city. It took them ten years. To help restore the Old Town to a perfect replica of its pre-war appearance, they resorted heavily to old photographs and even Canaletto oil paintings.

The Rynek has an intimacy lacked by some of its counterparts. Today it buzzed with street-café drinkers, artists, idlers like myself. Outside the cathedral - small, like that at Kraków, and rather austere - was a girl busking on the violin, and I sat on the steps to listen. After a few moments a stout, elderly nun came up and spoke to her severely. The girl stopped in mid-bar, packed up her fiddle and left. So I did the same.

A narrow street led to the Barbican, a red-brick gatehouse guarding a bridge across the moat between the double walls. Could all this mediaeval splendour really be less than half a century old? I bought an ice-cream and sat on the walls to watch the crowd, and exactly on cue the violinist reappeared and resumed her playing.

Back at the Rynek, the museum was showing a film of pre- and post-war Warsaw. To chronicle the destruction, it used footage taken from Nazi HQ immediately after the war: the blazing castle, the use of dynamite to level any bricks somehow left standing, all filmed with hideous pride in a good job well done. The post-war reconstruction, the cheerfulness and cameraderie of the rebuilders, were extraordinarily moving. Emerging afterwards into the daylight of the square, I saw it again as if for the first time.

*

On the eastern edge of Warsaw was a strange phenomenon: a road sign. Unfortunately it pointed to Bialystok and Augustów, and I didn't want to go there yet. Still, you had to be grateful that somebody had made the effort.

Getting out was the usual matter of map and compass. Actually, I didn't have a compass. A good job the sun was out. Again by luck I ended up on the right road; but as there was absolutely nothing to tell me so I sweated a bit until, fifteen miles or so further on, I hit the town I was aiming for.

The countryside here was flat and sandy, with large erratic pockets of forestry. One of these nearly proved my downfall, for while searching out a resting place I bogged the van in a big puddle of soft sand.

Jamming sticks and stones under the wheel was slowly improving the situation when a well-meaning cyclist stopped and insisted on trying to push. It didn't look promising, and by the time he admitted defeat and cycled cheerfully on, the van had been sucked in deeper than ever, with the sand now over the springs.

In desperation I began to try digging with my bare hands, and was making absolutely no progress when along came a knight in shining armour. Or, to be precise, a young man in shorts and a large rusty lorry. In no time at all he had fixed a tow rope and yanked the van safely back on to terra firma. Almost before I'd had time to thank him properly, he had revved up and disappeared in a cloud of exhaust fumes .

After that near-disaster I kept on the road until the terrain gave way to open, firmly grassed farmland, and stopped for the afternoon under some trees, with the day's labour going on all around.

As the sun dropped lower and the heat went off the day, gentler work gave way to ploughing. Across the road an elderly man began training a young horse to the plough. Meanwhile his wife kept an eye on two cows, tethered to the cart which had brought the whole ménage. Their dog trotted up and down the furrow, disappearing with yelps of delight when it put up a couple of partridges. A few yards behind the ploughshare followed two seagulls - and a copycat stork.

I asked the old man if I might photograph him. As he left his horse and came over to talk, his hands were shaking with Parkinsonism. We chatted politely for a few minutes, exchanging much goodwill while each understanding not a word the other said. Afterwards he returned to his work, his hands on the plough once again as steady as a young man's.

The travelling that followed was sheer delight. There had never been a lovelier afternoon, the light at its best with the westering sun behind. All around was an ocean of green, with just enough swell to make it interesting. Here the new leaves were fully out, apple and chestnut trees flowered profusely and the abundant dandelions added a splash of yellow to the verges.

Driving was effortless as the van ate up mile after mile on arrow-straight roads. The Romans might not have actually been here, but you could see where they may have got their ideas.

Very few tractors worked the fields, horses being almost universal. It took only one horse to turn this light soil. I thought of my old farmer friend Ted, who had worked the Gloucestershire clay with a team of three until the fifties; and after his retirement entertained us youngsters with stories of country life. He would have appreciated, and well recognised, these surroundings.

Even on the roads, nearly every vehicle that I overtook was a horse-drawn cart - often with a cow or two attached behind - and not just because this was all the van could catch. It was virtually all the traffic there was. The horses looked, without exception, in superb condition, all well in their coats, and all throwing their weight into their collars with enthusiasm.

The first town of any size was Wegrów, which had obediently taken on board a little industry and provided the requisite workers' tenements. At heart, though, it was still a country market town, as the size of the cattle market bore out. This probably represented the Metropolis for the farmers along the road, perhaps the furthest many of them had been in their lives.

Beyond, agriculture again gave way to forestry. The wide tracks and a number of partially cleared areas gave a flavour of Bovington, or Tidworth perhaps. Egdon Heath or Salisbury Plain? It was difficult to decide.

In one particularly beautiful village, a woman was milking a cow hard by the roadside, the squirt of white plainly visible in the instant of passing. Just beyond, the sign to Treblinka Concentration Camp was a shock, a reminder that life had not always been so tranquil. A rash of pillboxes suddenly sprouted along the route, reinforcing the thought.

Each village had its own distinguishing marks. One looked French, with pollarded trees. In the next, where they had suddenly caught the fashion, the trees were simply lopped, cut off in their prime like so many dwarf telegraph poles.

As I crossed the gloriously named River Bug, the sun was directly behind, and stayed glued in the mirror until it set. After this there was little more to see. This also included, of course, road signs. At the next town finding my way reached a ludicrous extreme, for I had to get out of the van and find the Pole Star before choosing a road out.

*

On Poland's eastern marches is the ancient Bialowieski Forest, reputedly the oldest surviving tract of primeval woodland that once covered most of northern Europe. Once a hunting forest for Polish and Lithuanian kings and Russian Czars, it is now Poland's longest established National Park.

Sixty-two species of mammals inhabit the forest, including elk and boar; but it is best known as the last home of the European Bison.

For me, though, there was something even more interesting here. I had come to see the horses brought back from the dead.

*

It felt odd to wake up in a proper bedroom, and at first I was disorientated.

I had arrived in Bialowieza rather late, and at the end of my strength. It was time for a bit of comfort. What's more, I was fed up with sticking to everything I touched, and both I and my clothes were in dire need of hot water. Although the hotel wasn't officially open yet, its people had kindly agreed to put me up.

The day spent getting to Warsaw, when I'd had no daytime rest, was having the usual delayed action. It was after mid-day when I left my room, with brain and legs barely functioning.

I had sent a letter ahead of me, asking to visit the Rare Animal Breeding Centre. The address, I now realised, was incomplete, and I hadn't had any reply. Once here, I was sure, I could find someone to tell me about the horses which I had come to see. At the moment, however, I wasn't capable of rational conversation, and must wait until my mind cleared a little.

In the centre of the village was the Park, the grounds of the earlier Palace, now housing the museum, a hotel and one or two hostels. It was a pleasant and undemanding place, and I idled by the lake until some of the rusty cogs in my brain began to turn and I could cope with the museum.

This was surprisingly big, with the lower floor given over to the vegetable and mineral content of the area, while the upper housed an extensive celebration of its animal life. There must have been a good many of the Forest's eleven thousand species represented here. I spent an hour wandering around its varied and sometimes gruesome exhibits: hideously snarling animals stuffed and mounted, butterflies spreadeagled and pinned to boards, bugs of every description and some that defied description. I didn't learn much, as the information was in Polish with no subtitles, but it was still fascinating.

Most interesting, from my point of view, was the tarpan. Smooth and rounded with the contours of a cuddly toy, it had evidently been stuffed by someone who didn't know horses. But it was a privilege to see the mortal remains of a creature that had been extinct for nearly two centuries.

An ancient type of horse that once roamed throughout the steppes of Europe and Asia, the tarpan was a primitive species probably related to the Przewalski or Mongolian Wild Horse, and to the ancestors of the domestic horse of modern times. Like the Przewalski, or their mutual cousin the zebra, it lacked docility and wasn't readily tamed. This made its value to Man minimal, except possibly to eat, and with gradual encroachment of agriculture and erosion of grazing lands, its habitat dwindled until there were only a few left in the environs of Bialowieza. Eventually these, too became history.

But the blood didn't die out entirely. The degree of genetic closeness to domestic horses made it possible to cross-breed. The tarpan itself may not have reckoned much to domestic work; but interbred with farm horses gave rise to a fairly serviceable animal.

It therefore produced descendants; and in some of these colour and type were well preserved. Before these became inextricably merged with those of domestic forebears, interest in reviving the breed began to grow. An extraordinary experiment was begun, which today has resulted in a thriving population of a horse that is the nearest living thing to the extinct tarpan.

It was to find out more about this experiment that I was anxious to visit the Rare Breeds Centre. But time was getting on, and I still didn't even know where it was.

The man in the nearby hotel was very kind and most keen to help. However, I was obviously making a bad job of communication. He gathered that I was trying to go somewhere, and led me round the back to a cellar. Here, like a conjuror coming up with a rabbit, he offered me a bicycle. Stuttering my thanks, and pink with embarrassment, I apologised for troubling him and beat a hasty retreat.

My luck was in, for I now stumbled into a party of English botanists whose guide was fluently bilingual. In no time he had directed me to the centre. "Ask for Professor Pucek."

Success at last. But the two conversations were the last straw, and I burned out suddenly and completely. I had to lie on a bench for an hour, waiting until I could stand up and walk. As for what to do next, it was Hobson's Choice: get back to the van and go to bed.

When at last some strength seeped back, I decided on information first, animals second; and drove to the Rare Breeds Centre to ask if I might see the Professor. But he wasn't here, they said. Moreover, as it was now late on Friday afternoon, he would probably be gone for the weekend.

Savagely I cursed The Beast, which had robbed me of the best part of the day and with it much of my reason for coming here at all. But my rantings were premature. A few moments later someone discovered that the Professor was out for the day, but would be in on Saturday morning.

Saved! I went back to bed and repeated the earlier dose.

*

Bialowieza's main street would have made a good set for a western movie. This was wooden house territory again, and those lining the long, straight dirt road were severely functional and a bit tatty. Now and again a horse ambled past drawing a cart. That was just about all the traffic there was.

Beyond, the road ran a few hundred yards on a converging course with the Belorus border, before turning back in a loop to rejoin itself: a lollipop route. A track led off at right angles to cross a small field before entering the forest, and I wandered down to take a look. It would be nice to add Belorus to my tally.

Just inside the trees a high wire fence stretched in both directions, and the path itself was blocked with a trench and mound. A Land-Rover and a couple of men were parked close by, and one at least wasn't out for a stroll; his fire and billycan gave him an air of permanence. Perhaps he was some sort of informal guard, to deter smugglers of the cheap Russian caviar which reputedly stocks the markets of Hajnówka and Bialystok nearby. If so, he didn't take his job too seriously, for he returned my greeting with indifference and made no objection as I passed.

The woods smelled good enough to eat: a sort of composite of damp earth, fresh leaves and wildflowers. This ancient forest was markedly different from those further west. The mix of trees was varied and random, the ground underneath matted with undergrowth, the diffused light only weakly breaking through the tangled canopy overhead. In the lighter parts by the track grew drifts of violets and stitchwort, with the yellow archangel just drawing breath ready to burst into flower.

I thought of Old Peter's Russian Tales; and as I looked over my shoulder for Baba Yaga or the Witch Baby, I was only half joking.

*

Professor Pucek was busy with the English botanists. I waited next door in a room where zoological books and journals crammed the shelves from floor to ceiling. The sunlight glancing off the polished table, the cooing of pigeons outside, were soporific.

Would the Professor have time for an importunate traveller, I wondered? But I needn't have worried. Patient and courteous, he possessed that deep-rooted enthusiasm for his subject that is a common thread linking all who work in Conservation. The small flame of my interest was more than enough to kindle that enthusiasm. With immense goodwill and genuine pleasure he spread his knowledge before me.

Professor Pucek attributed the preservation of the tarpan genes largely to an early twentieth century zoologist, one Professor Vetulani. It had often been observed that many farm horses in eastern Poland bore characteristics showing evidence of tarpan descent: the distinctive mouse-grey colour, the dark dorsal stripe, horizontal leg markings. The latter two signs they shared with some of the more primitive breeds of horse, including the Highland Pony and, notably, the Przewalski Horse. Professor Vetulani, together with some other breeders, collected as many of these throwbacks as he could find and established a breeding herd at Bialowieza. Unfortunately it became yet another victim to the Nazi occupation, as the greater part of the herd was removed to Germany. But after the war the remnants were collected together, and the experiment resumed.

The result is what is known as the Polish Primitive Horse - I mustn't refer to it as the tarpan, said Professor Pucek severely, for it was part domestic horse. Today there are more than a hundred, most of them in the Institute of Experimental Animal Breeding at Popielno, with small populations at one or two centres elsewhere. Although physically they closely resemble the original model, their domestic horse genes ensure a much more docile temperament. Many are used for farm work, some even as children's riding ponies.

Those at Bialowieza, however, live a life of idle luxury on the Reservation, an area of large fenced pens within the forest, which they share with the bison, wild boar and sundry less exotic creatures such as the odd deer.

I spent my last morning here, watching the older horses laze in the sun, while the youngsters obeyed their atavistic instincts in a series of battles and chases. A stallion and four mares made up the adult group. Each mare had a foal at foot - one hundred per cent fertility, claim the supporters of the breed - and one yearling remained from last season. He would soon follow his half-brothers and sisters to one of the other centres. With such a small gene pool, inbreeding is a constant threat.

It wasn't the same as watching animals in the wild. The bison, in particular, showed all the complacent idleness of knowing exactly where its next haynet was coming from. Most fun were the two wild boar, which cooled their blood in glorious mud while four or five brightly spotted, squealing piglets climbed all over them. The pen marked "Elk" was empty.

I went on my way at last, well pleased, heading northwards back through the forest. Just before I left it I had one last, long look at its wildlife. For a buzzard crossed straight in front of the van, then flew along beside me for some distance, dodging and jinking among the trees with no more than the lazy flick of a wingtip. Saying goodbye, or just escorting me off the premises?

CHAPTER XIV: THE MAZURIAN LAKES

Strange quest by perilous lands of marsh and brake

And circling woods branch-knotted like a snake

(Swinburne: Tristram of Lyonesse)

Hajnówka's bazaar was a damp squib. The other border guards must have been more zealous than those at Bialowieza, for there was no sign of the rumoured cheap caviar, or other smuggled Russian goods. But then, I suppose they would hardly have advertised the loot.

In reality, the market was little more than a rather grubby car boot sale, where you might buy, say, sweets and rusty nails from the same stall. But it gave me the chance to stock up on fruit.

I was now travelling north, roughly parallel to the border and heading for Augustów. Towards Bialystok I picked up a farmer's wife, cheerful, headscarfed and generously proportioned. She was also voluble, and in the end in desperation I tried her in Russian. It was a terrible mistake. At once she launched into a flood of heavily accented colloquial of which I couldn't understand one word in twenty. The more I urged her to speak slowly, the more she bellowed, leaning towards me and trailing clouds of garlic. It was an enormous relief when she yelled suddenly for a halt, and jumped out at a farm track. Afterwards, chastened, I switched off the Chopin which had been lightening the miles, and knocked some of the dust off my Russian tapes.

The countryside followed the now-familiar pattern of forest interspersed with agricultural land. Fruit blossom gave way to early lilac, growing indiscriminately in garden or hedgerow. Almost every house was of wood - the "Izba" which rules the architectural roost from here more or less to the Bering Strait.

A new feature was the large round stones, or piles of smaller ones, punctuating the fields at regular intervals: landmarks, perhaps? Further north a few railed paddocks appeared, completely altering the landscape.

Life here was slow-paced, with no visible urgency. On this Saturday afternoon, old men sat on the benches outside every house, watching the world and me go by. Piped water was evidently scarce, for even the newer houses had wells outside, usually traditional ones with windlass and roof; occasionally of the counterpoise type as in Hungary.

The influence of further east had crept in via the onion domes of the little wooden churches. The tiny village of Bohoniki, however, went one better with a wooden mosque. Hereabouts are pockets of Tartar population, people who have crept west over the ages since the Mongol conquest of Russia in the thirteenth century, collecting the Moslem faith somewhere on their way through Turkestan.

I almost missed Bohoniki altogether. Road signs were as scarce as ever, and when after driving in circles I found a village called Bobroniwki, but no mosque, I cursed my book for its inaccuracies. Then, with a sudden pricking of excitement, I found myself on a road signed "Tartar Way". Five minutes later I was there.

The mosque, rather dingy, was closed and deserted. As I was about to give up and go, a boy of about ten came running up. His round face and slightly narrowed eyes were unmistakeable. It gave me goose pimples to think that his forebears had ridden from the steppes of Central Asia with Batu and the Golden Horde.

The lad took me inside, and I removed my shoes to explore the heavily carpeted interior, exclaiming over the wooden mi'rab and chandeliers, like the furnishings of the little church at Zakopane. Koranic texts rambled over the walls. An upper gallery extended the seating, while a small, plain back room was set aside for lesser mortals... the females of the congregation. Before leaving I put an offering in the plate and gave the boy the rest of my small change. I couldn't help thinking of it as "Baksheesh".

I had wasted time getting lost and was, as usual, behind schedule. It was getting dark as I came back through Sokolka to begin the last leg of today's journey, and the rain that had been threatening for hours broke in a sudden drenching downpour that made it darker still. It was as I was leaving the village that I realised, with a sense of impending doom, that the uneven lurching of the van wasn't entirely due to the potholes and puddles in the road surface.

Which brings us back to where I came in.

*

Changing the wheel took me an hour, and during that time the rain was the only thing that stopped; at least a dozen cars passed by, but all on the other side.

It was more an IQ test than an exercise in basic mechanics. I loosened the wheel nuts by fitting the wheelbrace horizontally, climbing on to it, clinging to the ledge of the van roof, and bouncing precariously up and down until something gave; and fitted the spare by letting the jack down until the van was at ground level plus one millimetre, then literally putting my shoulder to the wheel. It was a messy job, not least for a river of sludge running under the exact centre of the van.

Afterwards, the only sensible thing was to stop there and then for the night. But the old anti-ME bloody-mindedness had a grip. My brain was too tired to react to a new situation, and instead clung doggedly to the old plan with the blind compulsion of an ant. Like a robot I climbed into the driving seat, turned the ignition key and started the conveyor belt. The nearest I came to lucid appraisal was in convincing myself that to pull off the road on to wet ground was to invite bogging down; a thoroughly specious argument as the storm was obviously local, and five miles further on the road was as dry as a bone.

I know, as it was every five miles that I got out and knelt to check the wheel nuts. I'd tightened them the same way as I'd loosened them, and every time I braked or cornered I nervously counted my wheels.

It was the first time since Germany that I had been on the road long after dark. The countryside was suddenly full of cats, darting across under the wheels, or crouching under the lilac bushes, visible only by amber eyes glinting in the headlights. Were cats particularly numerous in this corner of Poland, or just strictly nocturnal?

At last, half a dozen wheel-checks later, I was close enough to Augustów to feel the pressure was off, and stopped in the surrounding forest. The dark was no deterrent to the mosquitoes, which homed in like heat-seeking missiles while I cleaned my teeth.

*

It was a sticky night and morning, with the van hermetically sealed against the mozzies. At last a stiff breeze blew up around mid-day, discouraging the bugs and allowing for a spot of much-needed ventilation.

I was finally chiselled out of my comfortable indolence by the unwanted attentions of a motor-biker, sporting a set of antlers attached to the rear of his bike: a Polish Eddy Grundy fan? But if he hadn't got me moving, I would never have seen the Hen Harrier that flew up hard by my wheels two minutes later.

A quick nut-check, then I was sauntering on through some of the loveliest forest yet; well-spaced pine underlaid by a thick carpet of lily-of-the-valley, local equivalent of the English bluebell. Dotted among the trees were neat little wooden huts with benches for picnickers - although in this bug-infested region it was hard to imagine any static enjoyment without benefit of a suit of armour.

Augustów lies on the very eastern fringe of the Mazurian lakes, which stretch for a hundred miles to Olsztyn and beyond. The town derives its life-blood from the Augustów canal, a network of waterways of which only a small part is man-made, the means of export for the area's most abundant product... wood, of course.

The guide book was disparaging, but I liked Augustów, a neat little town with a shady square. Perhaps I was biased, for here was that rarest of Polish amenities, a conspicuous public loo. It was subterranean and evil-smelling; but you can't win 'em all.

Water, water everywhere... I followed a few false trails before finding the harbour. On the way I passed the town church, its congregation milling outside in Sunday best. It was hard to tell if the service was starting or finishing, for groups were entering while others left. It was like the organised chaos of a Syrian Orthodox service, a turn-up-as-you-please social affair.

I was in luck, for on the quay was a pleasure boat on the point of leaving. The cruise was one of the loveliest boat trips ever, a gentle potter around Lake Necko and a little way up the River Rospuda which feeds it.

Once very much a backwoods part of Poland, this is evidently now a favourite holiday resort, and possibly something of a rich man's playground. The two extremes were well illustrated near the harbour. Some dilapidated fishermen's huts, with steep pointed eaves to the roof, stood on stilts right on the water's edge; while smart new apartments nearby tried to copy their style, almost but not quite managing to carry it off.

I had worn long sleeves; but the breeze blew the bugs away. Sunlight streamed down with generous and unseasonal warmth, glittering on the surface of the water. The loudspeaker played jolly, thigh-slapping music, while the passengers, of multi-national origins, beamed goodwill at the world in general - and, in particular, at the lively Dobermann pup thieving from crisp packets.

It was a day when the world wore a kindly face.

*

Today, despite the horrors of the previous night, I was beginning to feel more at ease and in control.

Keeping to my programme had been a constant strain. Although I had tried to be fiercely realistic in laying my plans, an inevitable over-optimism had allowed a few optional extras to sneak in through the back door. I'd found the amount of driving harder than expected, and, worse, hadn't left enough time for heavy traffic or bad roads. And so throughout the trip I had continually arrived at my destination late and exhausted. This in turn meant a late start the next day, fuelling a vicious circle.

Consequently I had been as obsessed as in my normal home life with the urgency to get, and stay, on top of things. I was reminded, as so often, of the ants in T.H. White's "The Once and Future King", whose entire vocabulary for all good things, and all bad, consisted respectively of "done" and "not done". My itinerary, source of hope and anticipation before departure, and meant to be a framework only, was becoming a tyrant. The journey itself was in danger of turning into a grudging process of dourly ticking items off the list.

Just now, however, I was more relaxed and... what, exactly? If not quite restored, then at least held together for the moment with sticking plaster. I'd survived a problem without major disaster, and was beginning to lose some of the fear of getting behind. And with two-thirds of the journey accomplished, it seemed reasonable not to worry any longer about failing badly.

Moreover, tomorrow was a rest day; after that, there was the pleasant prospect of some gentle pottering around north-east Poland and the excitement of the Baltic states. A further psychological boost was that I had found someone to repair the kettle at last.

Was this hubris? I wondered, as I permitted myself a touch of satisfaction. But I would enjoy it while it lasted. It was in a buoyant frame of mind that I got off the boat to resume, literally and metaphorically, the driving seat.

*

Suwalki is the last town before Lithuania. Beyond lay very different country from the eastern forests among which I had spent the last week. Here, gently rolling hills were interspersed with green, fertile farmland and dotted with tiny villages and lakes, endless lakes; smaller here than to westward but making up in number what they lacked in size.

The evening was golden and the surroundings a delight. I set a course eastward towards Wiżajny on the Lithuanian border, passing through villages more Lithuanian than Polish. For these borderlands have for centuries been tossed back and forth between Lithuania and Poland in endless games of diplomatic tennis; and in fact for more than two centuries the two countries shared a federation under a single king, ruling in its heyday an empire stretching from the Baltic to the Black Sea.

The Lithuanians were the last people in Europe to convert to Christianity. Near Wiżajny is the rounded hillock of Cisowa Góra, once the site of their pagan rites and justly likened to Glastonbury Tor. It is not very big, less than a hundred feet above the surrounding farmlands and certainly no higher than the neighbouring hills. Yet it manages to be a landmark for miles around; for it is conspicuous by an air of something apart, a feel of having being dropped in a landscape to which it doesn't belong. A pliable imagination might invest the rocks beneath its smooth grassy hump with terrible secrets from the dawn of time: rites of Moloch, incantations from Mordor, the Deplorable Word.

At sunset, it was even more atmospheric than by day. I climbed it in creditable time, passing on the way up two local couples who had been indulging in a few pagan rites of their own; then sat on the top in complete solitude watching the sun sink below the horizon. You could almost feel the earth breathe.

A few miles south, antiquity is further represented by the burial mounds of the Jacwingians. Little is known of this ancient people, whose lonely scattering of barrows is in stark contrast to the high rise blocks of Suwalki, distantly visible over the next hill.

Nearby a patch of forest gave me somewhere to hide for the night in my now habitual manner. If the Jacwingian ghosts walked at night, I certainly didn't hear them.

*

Getting the punctured tyre repaired was a piece of cake. A friendly team of Suwalki mechanics in a back garden workshop mended it in minutes, tightened the wheel-nuts and checked the tyre pressures, all for next to nothing. While they worked, children outside in the road made dandelion chains and floated them down the stream in a sort of floral game of Pooh-sticks.

It was a glorious morning, fit successor to the evening before. I drove slowly through the town looking for the station, as it was rumoured that steam engines still served the little branch line up to the border.

There wasn't a steam engine in sight at the station, but I was grateful to find a tap there, and stocked up on water. Then to the supermarket for provisions, and I was ready for a siege.

South-east of Suwalki is Lake Wigry. The largest stretch of water for perhaps fifty miles, it is a popular spot for water sports. But it was something else which I was after; for there are said to be two colonies of beavers on the western shore.

Could I possibly find one of them? Since my illness, and especially now that my greatest talent was for sitting still, I'd built on a formerly desultory interest in watching wildlife. To see a beaver in the wild would be in a different class from observing fox-cubs and badgers.

It looked, to be honest, pretty hopeless. The lake must be ten miles long, and its deeply indented western shore double that. To find either colony would be like looking for a needle in a haystack; even an able-bodied person could spend a week tramping up and down without success. But I might never come

134

this way again, and had to give it a shot.

So photogenic was the landscape, I almost didn't get there at all, stopping every half mile at a dilapidated yet lovely farm, a mare with a new-born foal, a posturing goose waving a dandelion in its beak. Reaching a lovely sandy bay with a view across the lake to an island monastery, I almost cancelled the beavers in favour of a paddle and idleness. And was glad that I didn't.

Another half mile of rutted track, and the road ran out. The shore was fifty yards away down a bank, but I resolutely avoided it in favour of a path leading directly south. The map showed a river running into the lake from that direction, and, as every school child knows, beavers live on rivers, not lakes.

It was a wild goose chase. I got nowhere near a river, and couldn't even find a way back to the shore for the enveloping marshes. My tally of wildlife was a couple of herons, a red squirrel, a slow-worm and a red kite.

I was angry with myself for the waste of energy. But it was a pleasant expedition, and worth it for the flowers alone. Cowslips carpeted the wood, with lily-of-the-valley ready to flower in a week or so. Where there would have been brambles at home, here there was wild raspberry, and wild strawberry hiding in the grass at its feet. Water avens, various cinquefoils and bugle rioted happily, and honeysuckle was coming into early bloom.

The only drawback was, as ever, the voracious mosquitoes. I let my hair loose to save my neck and sank my hands deep in my pockets, but they found all the cracks, and chewed me where the sweat stuck my thin shirt close to my body. Back at the van, it was another hot, airless afternoon, with every door tight closed.

In the evening, I reckoned I couldn't leave without at least checking out the shores below the van. As I tackled the bank I saw something in the water, swimming strongly with its nose just visible, and leaving a distinct bow wave. I squashed my rising excitement with contempt: just a water rat.

From all quarters came the sounds of evening; hooting moorhens and the splash of fish jumping. Two cuckoos called from opposite sides of the inlet with imperfect pitch, one a full tone higher than the other. Soon a boggy patch barred the way, but something drove me on; there was a path of sorts, and somebody must have had a reason to tread it. Almost immediately both shoes filled with black sludge, and I cursed my folly. But there was now nothing to lose, so I went a bit further, and a bit further...

And suddenly literally choked with disbelief, for on the ground in front of me lay a tangle of small trees and saplings. Common enough in virgin wood at the end of winter. Only these hadn't been felled by storms. Their ends were tapered, chipped away... bitten through. Against all the odds, I had found my beavers.

A few steps more, and I heard a colossal splash. I looked across to the swan I had spotted a moment before, but it was still floating serenely, feathers unruffled. And as I waited, a dark shape surfaced and swam across my line of vision, not five yards away. Definitely not a water rat.

Carefully I raised my camera and took a photograph. At the click of the shutter, the creature dived, at the last moment flicking its broad, flat tail high and thumping the water with a loud Thwack! - the noise of a minute earlier. The show was over; it didn't surface again.

A few yards more, and I came on the lodge, a mound of bitten trees and brush among three large pines on the lake's edge. It looked too small to mean much, but a scraping sound filtered up through the twigs - Mrs. Beaver having dinner?

The mosquitoes were doing just that, with me on the menu. Anyway the light was failing; no point in staying any longer. On the way back I again saw the beast responsible for the original bow-wave; with hindsight, definitely not a water rat, but a young beaver.

Next morning all was deserted. The beavers had breakfasted early and gone back to bed. All around, though, it looked as if a couple of lumberjacks had been at work. A long trail of newly flattened grass led back into the forest, discarded spruce branches lying on it at intervals, and the shore at the end of this towpath was still wet with fresh mud. I had missed out on a spot of nocturnal tree-felling.

At the lodge, though, life went on. From below the pile of sticks came a mewing sound, a faint slurping and twice, unmistakeably, a burp. The younger members of the family were at breakfast.

I now had a serious decision to make. I was due in Vilnius the next day, at the office of the Lithuanian Equestrian Federation, and must not be late. By setting off this morning, as planned, I could make my leisurely way across the border, stop in or around Vilnius for the night, and arrive in plenty of time.

But I had seen so little of the beavers, and to do so was a once-in-a-lifetime opportunity which couldn't be missed. I now knew that they would be out and about in the evening; if I stayed until then, and hit the road at dusk, about eight, I could cover most of the necessary miles by elevenish. A still, small voice urged the idiocy of a late night before a specific appointment. It got ignored; if I rested all today, prolonging the evening by a couple of hours wouldn't kill me.

So I went back again to the van and, apart from a hairwash and a bit of tidying, dutifully spent the day horizontal. It was utterly quiet. I had now been here for twenty-four hours without seeing a soul, and even the bugs called a truce. The only thing that disturbed me all day was a hornet which flew in through one half-open door of the van and straight out, thank goodness, through the other.

At six I was back near the lodge, swathed in folds of clothing and sticky with midge cream. Hunkering down behind a tree on the lake's edge I disturbed a big fat toad, who wriggled with bruised dignity from under my foot. For the first hour the only other sign of life was a fox who ambled down from the forest, eyed me suspiciously for a moment, sat and scratched himself at length while he thought about it, then gave me a definite thumbs down and left. More time passed.

There's always a terrific thrill in seeing a shy wild creature come out of its den. You never actually see it emerge. One moment there is nothing, the next it is suddenly there, appearing without the help of a puff of smoke or even the blink of an eye, as if on a cleverly spliced piece of film.

Not that there was anything insubstantial about my beaver to explain his stealthy arrival. A big fat fellow, he sat sniffing the air as unconcernedly as if he had strolled into the picture in full view. He paddled around happily before swimming away and diving - cleanly this time, without the noisy tail thump. A little later he was back, climbing on to the shore and taking his supper from the poles above the lodge, using great yellow teeth to strip the bark with the same scraping sound that I had heard last night.

Afterwards he swam so close to me that I could see a great raw patch on his head behind one eye. Perhaps he had been in a fight; or, more likely, had been standing in the wrong place when he brought down last night's tree. I held my breath; but, moving slightly, snagged my sweater in the tree-bark with the faintest flick. And he was gone, with another tail-slapping splash.

I gave him fifteen minutes, but he didn't reappear. It was getting dark, and high time to make a move.

I found my way back through the tortuous tracks to the main road without a single wrong turning, then wasted the advantage in several circuits of Suwalki chasing petrol. It was quite dark by the time I reached the border at Szypliszki, and that was when things began to go wrong. For the border crossing - the only one on the map between Poland and Lithuania - wasn't there any more.

CHAPTER XV: LAND OF THE WHITE KNIGHTS

Visit rarely, and you will be the more loved.

(Arabic proverb)

Instead, an axle-crunching switchback of earth banks surrounded massive roadworks. Several hundred long yards further on was a barrier across what remained of the road; and that was it.

As I blinked in confusion, a man emerged from a nearby hut. He was one of the construction workers, and knew the score. The border, he said, was closed. There was a new crossing thirty miles to the south-east, beyond Sejny. Bad news. It meant another hour's driving - in the wrong direction.

It was now quite dark. The road twisted and undulated, often between high banks. It probably crossed more of the lovely, rolling hills that I had seen a couple of evenings before. I felt cheated. After a week of largely featureless plains, I wanted to enjoy the landscape, but it was invisible outside the narrow arc of the headlights.

Worse was to come. Despite the time of night, the new crossing held a queue of a hundred cars, creeping forward only every ten minutes or so.

It took three hours to cross. I filled the time with supper and a wash, spilling water as the queue inched ahead and making a damning puddle between my legs on the seat. When my turn finally came to go through, there was nothing to explain the delay; just a quick perusal of documents, and a nod. Perhaps I have an honest face.

But I was luckier than I knew. I later learned that it is far slower in the other direction. Smuggling goods out of Lithuania into Poland is a national sport, and vehicles may be stripped to the chassis on the least suspicion. It isn't uncommon for the crossing to take three days.

Once in Lithuania, my troubles were far from over. On the far side of the border lay six miles of unmade road. Ages passed before any road signs appeared with names recognisable from the map, and I dared not stop until I knew where I was, as there would be no time for getting lost in the morning.

When I finally pulled off the road, it was 3 a.m. And I was due in Vilnius, with all my faculties in working order, in just a few hours.

*

The office of the Lithuanian Equestrian Federation was on the first floor of a building occupied entirely by sporting organisations. On the door was a note saying, "Gone to lunch" - or words to that effect.

This was a great relief. After a very short night, shortened even more by an hour's time difference, I had driven furiously to reach Vilnius by just after midday, and was quivering with exhaustion. I left an answering note and went to recharge.

An hour later, the Federation Secretary was back. Mr. Mečislovas Preišegolavičius was a cheerful, ruddy-faced enthusiast with a twinkle in his eye which, it seemed, nothing ever dimmed. "Just call me Mr. Mečislovas!" he said, as I stammered my way through his surname. Lithuanian names, I was to discover, make few concessions to dimwitted foreigners, but this one was a baptism of fire.

With the help of Larima, a lady from the office next door who spoke fluent English, he sketched his ideas for introducing me to the equestrian world in Lithuania. I was particularly interested in native breeds; but first, he suggested, I might like to see something of the competitive side. There was a very good riding club in Vilnius. Perhaps we might start there.

Mr. Viktoras Milvedas, the Federation chairman, would join us later. I had two hours in which to change money and find a hotel. It sounded ample.

But it just wasn't my day. Of the four hotels on my list, two didn't exist, one had closed and the last was way outside my scope at eighty dollars a night. Sleeping in the van would hardly establish my credentials with the élite of Lithuanian equestrian society. I wondered if I could get away with a fictional hotel name and hide overnight in a back street.

Worse, I lost myself in the tangle of Vilnius roads, and was late again. Mr. Mečislovas dismissed my apology with a smile. He didn't even complain when we picked up Mr. Milvedas, and he himself had to climb into the back of the van and crouch amid the chaos of my unmade bed. I warmed to him even more.

We crossed the River Neris by the main bridge, picked our way through the labyrinth of the old quarter, and reached the edge of the city just where the bypass runs beside a wooded hill. A couple of hundred yards along a tiny lane shaded with lilac, and we arrived at the Club.

And what a club! I hadn't been sure what facilities to expect from a small, formerly Communist-run country; but these simply took my breath away.

Large indoor and outdoor schools, a separate showjumping arena, stabling for upwards of sixty horses, a big office block, a bevy of grooms... enough to rival Stoneleigh. But then, as I quickly learned, this was in fact the equivalent of the British Equestrian Centre, for it accommodates three top class coaches and two Lithuanian champions.

"Now," announced Mr. Milvedas after a tour of the stables, "we will go up the hill." A muddy lane led away through the trees to where afternoon training went on. And here was the biggest surprise of all, for only a mile from the centre of this busy capital city was a Garden of Eden for its riders.

On a plateau surrounded by woodlands, a massive natural arena filled perhaps twenty acres, with cross-country fences, a dressage area and ample space for training the entire Club simultaneously. National Coaches Alexandras Navickas and Kestutis Natkervičius were teaching young protegés in showjumping and eventing respectively. Only a few yards away a lesson for child beginners was in progress, and a young woman circled nervously on the lunge.

I was in luck, for both National Champions were at exercise. Alfredas Zuirblis warmed up the three-day-event winner Penatas before schooling over some fences. His dog, never more than a couple of strides behind, wore an infectious grin to rival his master's. Even Penatas, stopping to blow noisily through his nostrils, seemed to laugh with them. On the other hand Voldemauras Žukauskas, silent and impassive, was only walking quietly, for his showjumper Štormas had competed yesterday.

But for all the talent in Vilnius, Mr. Milvedas explained, just now the sport of riding as a whole was in a precarious state financially. No longer subsidised by the State, the Equestrian Federation couldn't afford to send competitors abroad for international experience.

Instead, he said, they were working feverishly to make opportunities for the opposition to compete against them at home. Lithuania already hosted a Volvo World Cup Qualifier at Raseiniai, with many central European countries represented; while in dressage, Vilnius would hold a competition for the new "Middle European League" in a year or so. They hoped to attract sponsorship to the sport by such high profile events.

Lithuania's affinity with the horse goes back a long way. Since the Middle Ages the emblem of the country has been a white knight on a white horse. Its history of those days reads like a mediaeval romance, with fierce battles against the Knights of the Sword and, later, the Teutonic Knights, both of whom were trying to impose Christianity on the last pagan country in Europe.

In this century equestrian strife has been purely sporting, initially much the preserve of the Army. With Soviet domination, however, riding was designated "an aristocratic sport for the enemies of the People" and almost entirely stamped out for a time. Interest crept cautiously back in the fifties, and tentative efforts were initiated to import breeding stock from Germany and Poland.

By 1983 the Lithuanian showjumpers were showing the Soviets the way, winning the USSR Cup for five of the next six years. Their best horse ever, the mare Dekoracija, ridden by Raimundas Udrakis, competed at the Seoul Olympics. Her performance elicited a West German bid of half a million Deutschmarks. It was turned down.

For she belonged to the State; as, still, do most of the horses at the Vilnius Riding Club - and at the other clubs and studs throughout the land. But this is gradually changing; must, indeed, change if equestrian sport is to escape from the financial impasse. Sponsorship, after all, can only take a state-owned venture so far.

Lithuania, formerly more tightly within the Soviet grip than the Warsaw Pact countries, is taking some time to lose its embarrassment over the idea of private ownership. As these inhibitions slowly fade, perhaps there will be scope for individuals to raise their own profile, and that of their country in the process. True in all contexts, this must apply supremely to the highly conspicuous field of competitive sport.

*

Over in the dressage arena was a representative of the New Order.

Judra Kašarina was for ten years Lithuania's Dressage Champion, and subsequently became National Coach in that discipline. Blond and petite, she didn't look strong enough to collect a big thoroughbred in lateral movements - nor old enough to have a son well into his twenties.

Today, she had only novices to train. Last year's dressage champion hadn't come from Vilnius. But among the horses in the school were some of her own; and in this she was breaking new ground.

Her business was embryonic as yet. But with unbroken horses cheaply available from Russia, constant demand for highly trained dressage horses in western Europe, and Judra's fund of skill in between, its potential was obvious.

A few private pupils helped her eke out a still precarious living. Among these was Eva-Christine, attached to the Swedish Embassy and here for eight months. When lessons had finished we rode together, taking two of Judra's horses back to the stables by the scenic route around the far side of the hill.

Eva-Christine had seen some interesting sides to diplomatic life. After a spell in Ethiopia during the civil war, she had helped to set up the Swedish Embassy in Zagreb during the Serbian-Croatian conflict. These experiences made Vilnius a haven of tranquillity; although after hours she preferred to flee the ex-pat social scene for the peace and unpretentiousness of Judra's yard.

Her funny little short-legged, long-tailed dog, rescued from starvation in Ethiopia, trotted behind us through the winding tracks. The area is called "Belmontas", and I didn't need any Lithuanian to get the drift. Full spring darkened the woodland. New leaves leaned down to brush our faces as we passed, and the first hawthorn I had seen raised thoughts of home. At intervals we came on cross-country fences. I longed once more for Tim; how he would have loved this!

Nearly home, we stopped to let the horses graze for half an hour, getting murdered by mosquitoes, and nearly losing a saddle when Eva's horse tried to roll. Afterwards, arriving at the stables, I was nonplussed. The Riding Club was nowhere in sight.

This was Judra's own yard, newly built. The cottage nearby which had come with the land was still run-down. Later, when she had time, she would move here from her flat, and renovate it; but the horses came first.

Judra conducted the business of evening stables trilingually, switching effortlessly into Russian for one of the grooms and English for Eva-Christine and me. When the horses were all watered and fed, she brought glasses from the house. We sat on benches in the yard, slapping the bugs and watching our shadows creep towards the old cottage; and talking, inevitably, of life in Lithuania since Independence.

Here, it seemed, the transition had been particularly hard. As so often elsewhere, a few had galloped into positions of wealth and power, while the majority were tightening their belts.

The country won the support of the world in its brave struggle to secede from the USSR. Afterwards, though, it wasn't sure how to make use of its hard-won freedom. Many of the former Communists in High Places were hanging on to their power; some openly, and some renouncing their former creed to pin a new label on old policies. And frequently the decision makers, while professing free enterprise, were, consciously or otherwise, locked into the rigid framework of entrenched Communist ideals.

There could be no better example of this last than Judra's own experiences. For in aspiring to own and deal in "private" horses, she had attracted covert disapproval and even open enmity from the equestrian circle.

The worst hostility came from the Lithuanian Mounted Police, based at the

Vilnius Riding Club. They were formed only three years ago, and no-one seemed quite sure of their function, least of all they themselves. Of one thing, however, they were quite certain: as representatives of the State, they were the moral and ideological guardians of the Club's integrity. The idea of privately owned horses was outside their experience, and therefore anathema.

Opposed to Judra keeping her horses at the Club, they made things as difficult for her as they could. "Can you believe it?" said Eva-Christine, "They turned off the lights in the indoor school, while Judra was in the middle of a lesson. So dangerous..." Here, then was the reason for the hastily built yard, the still uninhabitable cottage.

We raised our glasses to the new enterprise. "I think," said Judra with a laugh, "we are a republic of bananas!"

*

Asking me where I was to stay, Judra saw through my feeble inventions and invited me to her flat. I followed her several miles round the ring road to a residential area in the north-east. Here we parked side by side in a compound strongly fenced and watched twenty-four hours a day by guards - a measure against the soaring crime rate since Independence.

We ate a supper of "black" - rye - bread and locally produced spiced sausage, and drank "Likeris" liqueur out of glasses engraved with Lippizaner motifs. Then came the indescribable luxury of a hot bath, my first for over a month. Last winter - Judra shivered at the memory - Russia had cut off the oil supplies, and there was no heating. Now an agreement had been negotiated, and the central boilers functioned again, providing communal hot water to all the flats around.

The following afternoon Judra took me to visit the Vilnius stud at the nearby village of Riese. Its manager, Vincas Civinskas, was a retired showjumper and Judra's long-standing friend, whose career had for many years run parallel to her own. It was a pleasure to leave the city for cooler, forested roads; and to take a relaxed view of the countryside which I had earlier hurtled through without looking at anything but roadsigns.

Topographically, it was very similar to north-east Poland. But Lithuanian hands had left very different fingerprints. This was particularly so of the forest edges, here less regular and allowed to trail their skirts far into the farmland. The wooden houses might have belonged to anywhere east of Warsaw. Intermittently we passed a rash of new buildings - dormitory areas for the nouveaux riches of the last couple of years, maybe.

Vincas gave us a warm welcome, and carried us off at once to see the horses.

As at the Riding Club, they were kept under the Soviet system - rows of stabling inside long barns, here beautifully formed from stone patterned with brick, and inscribed with a date from last century.

The English thoroughbreds were Vincas' favourites. With great pride he showed us the stallion Athens Wood (Afensvud, said his nameplate), whom I remembered from his racing days at home. Next came the Arabs, among them the descendants of two Egyptian Arabs, Aswan and Nila, presented to Kruschev three decades ago by President Nasser.

The following section brought a surprise. Among a mixed bag of mares and youngstock I found myself face to face with half-a-dozen Shetland ponies, far from home. But it was the last block which housed what I had wanted to see most of all; for Lithuania boasts one of the oldest breeds in the world, the Žemaitukas pony.

History records the Žemaitukas as far back as the thirteenth century. Believed to be descended via Tartar ponies from the Mongolian Wild Horse and later influenced by Arab blood, it was used in mediaeval times as a warhorse, and subsequently allowed to degenerate into a draught animal. At the beginning of this century, said Vincas, thousands were exported to Britain for use as pit ponies.

His two Žemaitukas stallions differed considerably. The first, the fourteen-year-old Argentas, was small and black, of about thirteen hands. His stable companion Novatorius was about fifteen hands, dun with dorsal and leg stripes, of appearance somewhere between a Highland pony and a Welsh Cob. These stallions represented the two extremes of "type". Whereas Argentas was of the older, purer strain, that of Novatorius was, it seemed, the more popular, injecting a size and substance suitable for both riding and driving. They don't reckon much to ponies in Lithuania, and child riders are usually put straight on to horses to learn.

Outside, a small, jovial man joined us. He packed us into his big, black Zil, a solidly-built car of Soviet design which he called his Russian Tank. Well-named, it bounced importantly along a rutted, pot-holed track to where thoroughbred youngstock grazed alongside Žemaitukas ponies.

It was a glorious spot. The hillside sloped down to a lake, then rose again to a newly built village, picked out in every detail by the evening sun glancing off the water. Virgin forest surrounded it on three sides: a harmonious blend of ancient and modern.

We bounced back over the pot-holes in the Russian Tank and finished the tour in Vincas' office round a bottle of Amaretto liqueur. One of his best horses, the Arab stallion Prizrak, had that very day been exported to Belgium. The bottle circulated rapidly as we drank to his health and fertility. It did me no good to plead that I was driving; Vincas' friend kept sneaking me a refill when I wasn't looking.

It was quite some time before Judra and I staggered out, to be met right on cue by a Žemaitukas-drawn pony trap. It might have been a good idea to offer the van for a straight swap.

*

After the unpromising start, Lithuania was turning out to be great fun. At last it was possible to get below the surface, to see how the New Order was working out.

What was more, my experience of the country was more sociable than any so far. True, I'd been "borrowing" hours as if there were no tomorrow, and was slowing up badly in every faculty. But my mounting debt could wait, for the opportunities here were too good to be missed.

So it was a pity that I chose this moment to put my foot in it... right up to the armpit.

The day got off to a bad start. Low on petrol, I tried out the old Soviet hobby of queueing at the only garage I could find. After only a quarter hour I bottled out, decanted my last spare gallon and hurried on into Vilnius, where I was due at the Equestrian Federation office.

Once again I got lost, not in the labyrinth of the old part but on well-signed bridges and main roads, where there was no excuse. Late, I missed Mr. Mečislovas, and wasted another half-hour in concocting a letter for him in laborious, excruciating and certainly incomprehensible Russian; and was later than ever when I finally arrived at Judra's stables to take her out to lunch.

She had changed into a dress for the occasion, and I cringed in my rugger shirt and jeans. When she discovered, though, that she had forgotten to change her shoes and had come out in flip-flops, we declared honours even, and bumped over the cobbles of central Vilnius in high good humour.

Leaving the van on Pilies Gatvė, the "Hill Street" that runs through the heart of the old town, we took a narrow alley and came by a spiral stairway to the brick vault of the Bear Restaurant. Starting with elk pâté - the nearest I ever succeeded in coming to an elk - the meal grew into a feast of mediaeval proportions, and we rolled out very much later in excellent cheer; whereupon I committed my act of imbecility by putting my rucksack down on the pavement to unlock the van's triple defences... and driving off without it.

It was catastrophic. The bag contained all my Lithuanian money and the last few days' diary; and, worse, all my exposed film so far, which I had decided not to leave in the van but to keep on me - for safety. And the spare keys for Judra's flat.

When I realised, much later, what I'd done, Judra was a tower of strength. She led me back to the restaurant, around nearby shops and kiosks, and finally through the dismal formalities at the Police Station. By the time we had finished, her whole afternoon was gone.

Back at the yard that evening, Eva-Christine was scathing. "You're an experienced traveller; you should know better!" She was absolutely right.

Nothing more could be done, except wait, and hope. Meanwhile, I had caused enough trouble. It was high time to make myself scarce. On the excuse of doing some sightseeing, I took the first road out of Vilnius, and fled.

*

The village of Trakai lies just a few miles west of the capital. Its mediaeval castle, perched on a low island in the middle of a lake, might have sprung from the pages of Malory or William Morris.

The Grand Duke Gediminas, last pagan ruler in Europe, moved his capital here in 1321. The castle was built soon after for defence against the Teutonic Knights, who considered the pretext of evangelism as a good opportunity to indulge in a bit of pillage and rape.

The style, Gothic dressed in red brick, was to become familiar as I crossed the Baltic states. At first sight it seemed pure fantasy, a jumble of tiled, conical towers rising straight out of the lake and reiterated, upside down and flickering, in the water below. Most was heavily restored; a not-so-old photograph in one of Judra's books showed a ruin. Kruschev, it was said, deplored the restoration, warning that Lithuanian Nationalism was a threat to Communist power and should be strenuously discouraged. Recent history has shown his fear to be well-founded.

Two wooden walkways led across a small island to the gatehouse, a square tower standing in the largest remaining section of original stone. The featureless quadrangle inside was as far as I got, for since losing my rucksack I had no tallonas to pay the entry fee - dollars were fine for the hawkers outside but refused by the *kassa*.

No great problem. Serious sightseeing definitely wasn't on the agenda today, and it was much more pleasant to wander around the outside. I sat and watched the boats, which ranged from yachts down to paddleboats. The water was crystal clear and I briefly felt the temptation to swim; but resisted it without too much difficulty.

Trakai's other castle was more to my liking. It stood on a slight rise in the town, where the ground had managed to heave itself into a tiny hummock before slumping back exhausted to another lake on the far side. No restoration here; among crumbling stone, the odd bit of wall or gatehouse had been maintained for living in, a haphazard but natural process of evolution.

Not far away was the kanissa, or prayer house of the Karaites. At less than four hundred, this is the smallest of Lithuania's mosaic of ethnic groups. Culturally they are something of a mosaic themselves: a Jewish sect with a mixture of Tartar blood and a Turkic language. History doesn't record why Gediminas' son Kestutis brought them here from the Crimea around 1400; but has since then celebrated their gardening skills - and their reputedly excellent pies.

I could have done with one of those. I was due back in Vilnius at four, though, and the day has a way of being short when you don't get out of bed until early afternoon.

For once I was in good time to meet Mr. Milvedas. My reward was excellent news: my rucksack had been found.

Judra's son, Edgaras, had had the inspiration of contacting the local radio station, who had put out news of my loss. Almost at once someone phoned in, to say that he had found it and taken it home.

"Home" turned out to be Elėktrėnai, thirty miles west of Vilnius. Judra, busy as she was, insisted on coming with me. With no Lithuanian, she said, I'd never find the place. Also, she was worried about her keys. Although she was too polite to say so, she didn't mean to give me enough rope to hang myself over again.

And she was right; I would never have managed alone. Elėktrėnai was an industrial town, every street of whose monster high-rise flats looked exactly like the last. There were no street names and the block numbers didn't run consecutively. Even the residents - and Judra stopped a good dozen - knew nothing of local geography beyond their own particular monolith.

It took us half an hour to find the right block. Mercifully, the flat was only on the second floor of a possible nine. As we entered, I gasped with astonishment. It was beautifully, almost richly furnished, with valuable ornaments and shelves lined with books. The contrast with the outside couldn't have been more marked.

The bag and its contents were intact. The young man had seen me drive off and picked it up at once. I was almost incoherent with gratitude, and was glad that Judra was there to translate.

It was nearly midnight when we got back. I was seeing double and my hands were, frighteningly, numb to the wrist. This drive was the biggest endurance test of the whole trip.

It was worth every minute.

*

The next morning, we were due to go our separate ways; I to Latvia and Judra to look at some horses for sale in Poland. When I went "up the hill" to take my leave of her, she was squeezing in one last lesson, with two bouncing German girls.

"Bouncing" in more ways than one. Both of large girth and enjoying the heatwave clad only in shorts, plimsolls and boob tubes, they clung to the saddles, barely able to manage a slow trot on the lunge. "Everyone rides dressed like this at home!" they gurgled happily.

Strong stuff for a National Coach; but a client is still a client, and must be humoured.

The unacceptable face of Lithuanian capitalism, perhaps?

CHAPTER XVI: LIV AND LETT LIVE

A KNIGHT ther was, and that a worthy man,

That from the tyme that he first bigan,

To ryden out, he lovede chyvalrye,

Trouthe and honour, fredom and curteisie.

In Lettowe had he reysed and in Ruce...

(Chaucer: The Prologue)

It was good to be an anonymous tourist once again, with no immediate destinations or deadlines. And it was as such that I spent a last, leisurely day in Vilnius.

This is not exactly a country whose history is writ large in text-books on Europe. Perhaps it is the distance of its obscurity that lends enchantment. There was an Arthurian thread running through my hazy concepts of Lithuania; scraps of knowledge of fact and symbol making it into a present-day Lyonesse, a land of ancient forests inhabited by wolf and elk and peopled by pagan knights on white horses.

Legend says that Nero sent expeditions to the "Amber Coast" in search of "sunstone", or amber. But it is hard fact that Baltic amber graced the Temple of Artemis at Ephesus, one of the Seven Wonders of the Ancient World.

Over the first millennium AD the Lithuanians and Letts drifted into the Baltic lands from the east. The latter gave their name to Latvia, where they settled; and also, confusingly, to Lithuania, whose native name is Lietuva.

It wasn't until the twelfth century that the outside world began to take an interest, with the arrival of traders from Germany. Soon after began the Baltic Crusades, a movement led by the Roman Catholic Church to Christianise the pagan Balts.

Thus arose the Order of the Knights of the Sword. The Teutonic Knights who later joined the campaign were a rather more professional bunch who had cut their teeth - and plenty of other people's - in the Holy Land.

For this was the age of Crusading. Decline in Palestine by no means weakened enthusiasm for the general idea of beating the heathen. After all, there were still the Albigensians in southern France and the Moors in Spain to see off, as well as the Balts. It became quite fashionable for debutant knights - including the future King Henry IV of England - to do their season in the Baltic, pushing back the frontiers of the Holy Roman Empire and learning their craft in the process. It was against such as these that Gediminas entered the history books, as Lithuania's first Hero.

As well as Trakai, Gediminas began the castle in Vilnius. At any rate it bears his name, but mostly post-dates him by a few decades. The castle was now in the throes of being "restored" - in other words, rebuilt - but the Gediminas Tower was original.

Inside was a small but well-furnished history museum with various lithographs and a few early artefacts. A sixteenth century map of the town showed it then of considerable size, with buildings straggling well outside an already extensive city wall. By this period Lithuania's Golden Age was over and its fifteenth century empire beginning to disintegrate, but Vilnius was still one of the biggest cities in eastern Europe.

Today its limits are well out of sight from the tower. Despite its size, though, the city has an intimacy rare among eastern capitals. The centre has no tall buildings to obstruct the view, which is further softened by abundant greenery - and the curvaceous lines of its many churches. Among its "narrow, cobblestone streets," said the poet Czeslaw Milosz, is "an orgy of the Baroque, like a Jesuit outpost somewhere in Latin America."

The Cathedral, immediately under the tower, is Neo-Classical. Dedicated to St. Stanislaus and housing a chapel to Lithuania's only native saint, St. Casimir, it has had an eventful life. Used as a garage in Stalin's time, it was later promoted to art gallery and finally reconsecrated in 1989.

Now, however, it was closed again - if only for the next three hours. Outside, a line of orange robes made its way across the square, to the accompaniment of chanting: a Hare Krishna procession. A few years ago they would have been as rare as Martians. Now they were just another symbol of the new Lithuania.

The tiny streets around, purgatorial during my earlier hurried transit by van, were paradise on foot. Except on Pilies Gatvė, hardly a single vehicle disturbed the dust. Not a hundred yards from the busy square were secluded cobbled yards, empty but for washing and woodpiles, and guarded by heavy doors. I stopped at a baker's for bread, and the assistant counted out the change on an abacus. Its two unused columns at the end baffled me, until I worked out that they were for hundredths of a tallonas - about 1/800th of a penny!

Back on wheels, I pottered up the leafy main street called, predictably, Gedimino Prospektas, to the Parliament building at the end. This was where it was all happening in 1991.

Along with much of western Europe I had sat glued to my television set, cheering on the infant Lithuanian government in its heroic stand against the Goliath of the USSR. Fourteen lives were lost when Soviet troops stormed Parliament and the TV building during their attempt to bring the Lithuanians to heel. But the government stood firm in its demand for independence until Gorbachev, not daring to squander the recent and fragile goodwill of the West, backed down. Today, scarcely a breeze disturbed the tranquil play of the fountains, and the violence was hard to imagine.

Looking for the Post Office, I wandered by mistake into a bookshop, and wandered out much later heavily weighed down. Among some cheap paperbacks was a glossy hardback on Lithuania, irresistible at 25p.

Unfortunately it was pre-democracy and a eulogy of Communism from cover to cover. It told me all I had ever wanted to know about the socialised production planning on collective farms, the industrial output of prefabricated concrete structures, and the 139 holders of the honarary title of Honoured Economic Rationaliser of the Lithuanian Soviet Socialist Republic. On history it was just a tad short, condemning the "penalties imposed on more than 6,800 people... for their revolutionary and anti-fascist activity" by the "bourgeois" government preceding Communism, but forgetting to mention the quarter million Lithuanians killed or deported in the years immediately following the Soviet takeover.

Heavy stuff. I gave up, tossing it on to the mattress in the back of the van. It would make good bedtime reading that afternoon, as it would certainly send me straight to sleep.

*

No Lithuanian heroes or Grand Dukes grace the main bridge over the Neris River. Instead there are statues of worthy Soviet comrades: a po-faced mechanic wearing overalls and wielding a spanner, a head-scarved peasant girl with a sheaf of corn and lamp-post legs.

I got to know them quite well by the time I crossed the river yet again, as I said farewell to Vilnius by getting routinely though only moderately lost for the last time.

My zig-zag exit took me through genteel suburbs, shaded and coloured by hawthorn, lilac and apple trees, now rather crumpled under the hot sun. Here, maybe, the upper crust had lived before the days of Stalin, although now the paint was flaking and the window frames sagging on their graceful wooden houses. Possibly even now Miss Havisham figures squinted out from behind moth-ridden lace curtains, brushing off cobwebs while they dreamed of the heady days of their youth, before their world caved in about them.

My navigation was partly excusable, for driving here was hairy. Despite the light traffic, it was often necessary to dodge unpredictable drivers, and traffic lights obeyed some very odd rules. Even an empty road kept you on your toes. Local road re-surfacing is done in two stages a week apart, leaving a hole in the road like an inside-out speed ramp - and producing much the same effect when you hit it at speed.

I found a petrol station with petrol and no queues, and filled up with super-91-octane before hitting the road to Latvia. With a twinge perhaps of guilt, Vilnius gave me up gracefully, dropping me neatly on the motorway without further ramblings.

The van seemed glad to be on the open road again. Before a following wind it galloped along like a restive horse on its stomach full of rotgut petrol, and it was hard to keep the speed below seventy as it ate up the miles to Riga. Wooden farmhouses were scattered across the landscape in familiar pattern, but here gaily painted in a variety of colours like beach huts. Occasionally a new brick house had demoted the old wooden one to barn - or perhaps, occasionally, granny flat.

The patches of cultivation formed small islands in a surrounding dark green sea. Forests cover one-third of the country, and lynx, boar, wolf and elk still live deep within them.

The "motorway" to Riga and Tallinn soon became a single track. Alongside ran a gravel path, obviously wanting to be a second carriageway when it grew up. A hundred miles out of Vilnius an accident stopped me: one car badly damaged and another on its side, leaching petrol dangerously on to the road. There were no serious injuries, but three passengers were badly cut about.

I was well stocked with water and medical kit, and stopped to help mop up. The victims wore that peculiar unfocussed gaze that shock brings. One minute they would clutch at the sponge and wipe their own skin with the the random movement of a small child; the next, sit passive and unaware while I cleaned off the worst of the blood. At long last the ambulance arrived, and they were whisked off to hospital.

I was left with a problem: no water remaining, and the urgent need of a wash. Also, the van was by now beginning to hiccup on the rubbish it had been drinking, and needed a top-up with real petrol. So I left the motorway at

Panevėžys, and went hunting.

The service station attendant was most helpful, and willingly spared me some water. A pity I got my buckets mixed up; but I still felt cleaner than before as I set off through the town and back to the road.

The traffic lights here were the most unusual yet. Their change directly from red to green kept catching me flat-footed, holding up the other cars, until I worked it out. A small electronic display panel at the side gave a count-down over the last five seconds, so that the initiated around me could get a flyer.

While in town - the last before the border - I needed to unload my last tallonas. It was Sunday, and only an off-licence was open. I couldn't drink while travelling, as alcohol would affect me for too long. But decent liquor could always be taken home. I hesitated between Crème de Cacao and Whisky with a beautiful Lippizaner motif on the label; but chocoholics will out, and I plumped for the first. For the last of the small change I stopped at the church and put it in the collecting box. I was glad I'd done so, for the interior was beautiful, with much rich, rather archaic silver plate, and wide soaring arches.

That afternoon I stopped for well under the four hours, anxious to press on over the border and get an early night. Fate, however, had other ideas. At the barrier was a queue stretching back a quarter mile: a last kick in the teeth, I thought grimly, from bloody Lithuania.

It took nearly four hours. Ironic to inch past a 70kph speed limit sign, at which the dachsund from the German car in front registered contempt in the time-honoured way. By a way-side cross the carved Christ figure, head in hand with a look of utter boredom, had obviously seen it all before.

At the post there was no fuss, no search, nothing to account for the interminable delay. "Danke schön... Auf wiedersehen!" said the guard pleasantly. I gave him back the last, adding in English, with a polite smile, "Not if I can **** well help it!"

*

The old countrywoman had a face of infinite serenity, her deep-set eyes brimming with good humour and kindliness. She spoke Russian with a soft lilt, and for once I could understand her.

Late last night, looking for a few trees to hide among, I had camped in a thicket on the edge of her farmland. But she welcomed me as guest, not intruder, and stopped to chat for some minutes before departing for her wooden izba, calling heaven's blessing on the remainder of my journey. With such an introduction, Latvia couldn't fail to be a friendly country.

Although that didn't stop me from making the almost obligatory hash of getting round Riga. The main street, named for Lenin, had like so many others changed its name - since democracy, they say here, you go to bed in one place and wake up somewhere else - but that was no excuse for making an unscheduled about turn and re-crossing the River Daugava before getting a grip.

Latvia is the most industrialised of the Baltic states. This is reflected in much of Riga, most of which is functional, grimy and unprepossessing. At its very core, however, the heart of the old Hanseatic town was unspoiled.

German merchants first arrived here in force in the twelfth century. In the next fifty years they incorporated Riga into the Holy Roman Empire and installed a Bishop; he in turn set up the Order of the Knights of the Sword to push back the frontiers of Christendom. The first people thus displaced were Livs, a Finno-Ugraic race, and thus more closely related to the Estonians than to their more immediate Lettish and Lithuanian neighbours; those, like most of Europe, being Indo-European.

In 1258 the town joined the Hanseatic League, that formidable alliance of German merchant towns which controlled trade in the Baltic and North Sea from Tallinn to York and beyond. Even now, three hundred years after the decline of the Hanse, Riga's architecture, with its solidly worthy red brick towers, walls and churches, is more Germanic than east European.

There is a token vestige of its early fortifications in a stretch of old city wall, much restored. Nearby is the Powder Tower, the last tower remaining and used in turn as arsenal, prison and - reputedly - torture chamber. From here the Swedish Gate led me into the old quarter through a jumble of the narrowest streets I had ever seen, and whose ancient houses had aged and evolved with contempt for plumbline and spirit-level.

This wasn't going to be a long tour. The stresses of Vilnius were beginning to bite deep, and every step was a wade through treacle. I just made it to a cafe near the river, where I got change in Latvian Roubles for my dollars. The orange I bought there, the first I'd seen for weeks, was purple inside, and after one doubtful taste I ditched it. But the roubles were precious, as for now they would save the legwork of hunting for a bank.

As I lounged at my table trying to find reasons for not going on just yet, I couldn't decide what I thought of the nearby Vansu Bridge. Cobwebs of fine steel drifting about its single pylon, it looked like something out of the next century. It was a pity about the stench of the water flowing beneath to the Gulf of Riga, the most polluted bay in Europe.

I trudged back to base via the Cathedral. Maybe the circumstances weren't ideal today, but it seemed to me the least attractive of the many I'd seen so far, its squat, dark brickwork only just redeemed from ugliness by a slender Gothic tower. No great disappointment that it was closed, although I should have liked to hear its excellent organ. Instead I sat awhile in the cheerful, bustling square outside, joining in with the universal occupation of watching the world go by.

And again in the small garden outside the Concert Hall, where artists sat at work under the shade of flowering trees. The Hall, once a guildhall for the Hanse, was officially closed, but I managed to slip inside and peer through the doors of the main hall for a glimpse of its fine mediaeval architecture.

And so to the van, where I collapsed gratefully into bed and spent the afternoon just where I was, on a busy main street in the middle of Riga.

*

I was roused in late afternoon by a cavalcade with limousines and police. Blaring with sirens and oozing with self-importance, they might have belonged to an African or Middle Eastern republic. In honour of the VIPs, whoever they were, a military band struck up. Heaving myself into a more or less vertical position, I went to listen.

Old Riga was surrounded by a moat, connected at both ends with the River Daugava. It lives on today in a series of long, thin lakes, surrounded by parkland. Between the claustrophobic streets of the old quarter and the hubbub of the modern city, it forms a peaceful oasis.

A nightingale had been singing there all afternoon, its ringing tones clear above the hum of distant traffic; but now the band had stolen the stage. Their performance was concert class, and in no time a large crowd had gathered. It was no surprise to hear that the snatches of conversation between each number were mostly in Russian; at 50% - over 70% in Riga - Latvia has the largest concentration of Russian ex-pats in the Baltic states, a situation which is beginning to cause considerable friction.

But the ex-pat to whom I found myself chatting was a different kettle of fish. An Indian-born American, he was a business consultant seconded from his university to spend two months as an adviser in Riga.

"What the former Soviet countries need," he said decisively, "is not so much western money as western know-how." With no experience of how to run a market economy, he went on, they were doubly hampered by inflexible attitudes. "Can you imagine," he said, "that in every ex-Soviet republic I've ever been in, from Siberia to Central Asia, the administration switches on its winter heating on November 15th!"

On the way out of town I passed the posh Hotel Roma. My water supply was very low; so I shamelessly stopped in its private car park, entered at the main door - held open for me by a liveried flunkey - and asked the receptionist for information I didn't want, before going as if on an afterthought into the cloakroom and loading up with half a gallon.

At the Roma I found the first English paper I'd seen for weeks; and even managed not to wince at the price, which was two dollars. Considering the water and their time, that was fair enough.

*

From Riga it was a scant thirty miles up the Gauja River valley to Sigulda. Here a gorge with a couple of ruined castles makes the spectacular setting for a holiday resort, health spa... and, at a maximum thousand feet above sea level, a winter sports centre.

Riga was even worse off for road signs than Warsaw. There was a sign to Tallinn, then nothing. The road turned left, then left again, until I was sure I was going south. The sun was well hidden; I could always wait for the stars, I thought irritably, and regretted quite seriously my lack of a compass. Eventually I turned off by instinct, and found myself luckily on the right road - and just before a petrol station selling 98E! E for excellent, or just edible? Either way, it would be a bit more dilution for the Vilnius rotgut.

The next sign, miles further on, appeared just after I'd lost my nerve and turned off again, this time wrongly. It meant an illegal U-turn followed by a sort of Latvian-style Spaghetti Junction, with roads shooting off in all directions at random. Instead of the usual concrete jungle there was an impenetrable screen of trees, which helped the orientation no end.

These were spectacular forests; mile after mile of thick larch, spruce and birch. At one point the two carriageways drifted a hundred yards apart. The odd farmstead stood folornly in between, more cut off from the outside world than if there had been no road for miles.

Sigulda itself sprawled through alternate forest and clearing, making it hard to find even the river, let alone the village centre. Eventually I found a board bearing a large map. Bilingual in Latvian and Russian, it was slow work to interpret. But at least, when I hid away in the forest that night, I had some idea what to look for the next day.

*

Next Day, however, looked ominously likely to be cancelled.

I woke up feeling much the same as on the first day in Poland, with hardly enough strength to sit up. Fringe benefits were a sore throat, a revolving head and a bed wringing wet with sweat. There was nothing to do but wait.

Patience paid off, and after mid-day I was at least partially mobile. Now that there was plenty of water, I washed everything in sight, starting with myself and ending by scalding the bowl I had used at the accident. Having thus re-asserted my control, I got back into bed and prepared to tackle some serious thinking.

More than anything else I was enraged, so close to the end, to find the last of my strength failing prematurely. The fact that it was my own fault, for loosening the strait-jacket too freely throughout - not to mention the extra mileage and stress caused by my piece of idiocy in Vilnius - was no consolation whatsoever. Simply, I had run the early laps too fast. Now that I needed to kick for the tape, I was up to my knees in treacle.

But to lie up for even one day now would tighten the pressure exerted by my deadline of the Tallinn-Helsinki ferry, leaving little or no time left to see my last two countries; whereas to push straight on - assuming I could - would very likely mean wasting the effort, by travelling through in a robotic state of exhaustion. It was a rotten dilemma.

"You hit a brick wall" a fellow hurdler had once commented, referring to the point where you turn into the last hundred metres with the fuel tank already empty, and two more flights rising like the Berlin Wall in front of you.

Well, I was now in sight of the finish, and sure enough had hit my brick wall. But it wasn't, I reckoned, as solid as the one I had hit crossing the Tatras. There were definitely a few cracks in the mortar. It was Plan B. I was going to put my head down and bash my way through; and climb somehow the last two hurdles of Latvia and Estonia, if I did it on my knees.

*

Again, the weather approved my decision. The Latvian sun doesn't always shine on the righteous - later that year it rained buckets on the Pope - but it gave me the red carpet treatment with blazing sunshine.

Opposite Sigulda on the north side of the Gauja River is its twin village of Turaida, where the first Bishop of Riga built his castle. In the car park outside, souvenir sellers were hawking their goods: mostly amber (rather expensive) or amber-coloured plastic (cheap and nasty), with a few items of wood-carving, including real and miniature walking sticks.

At the castle kiosk I confidently asked for my ticket in Russian. Unfortunately the lady at the till, who didn't know that I had spent half an hour rehearsing my few words, decided I needed a guide and dispatched a Russian student to take me round. I was in no condition for company, still less for conversation - in any language - but couldn't escape without seeming, indeed being, rude. Eventually, shameless in my desperation, I managed to slip the poor girl in the museum.

Begun in 1214, the castle was still in use in the eighteenth century when lightning hit the gunpowder store, and everything went up in a cataclysmic explosion.

It remained in pieces for nearly two hundred years. But today's Letts, like the Lithuanians, rebuild on ruins. Turaida Castle was reminiscent of Trakai, with fresh white mortar securing the red brick (most of which was also brand-new) above stone foundations of such age that they seemed fused into the bedrock. Scaffolding crawled over the walls; any ruined bits which had escaped "restoration" were hygienically sealed with cement.

Nothing, though, could diminish the position. Set high above the Gauja gorge, the castle commanded views for miles up and down the river. The ancient Livs, early settlers in the valley, named the place well: in Livonian, Turaida means the Garden of the Gods.

Sigulda, a mile away, was buried in trees; but a corner of its castle was just discernible on the edge of the scarp. Visual communications between the Knights of the Sword, who built there, and the Bishop's men must have been excellent. But getting there by road was a different matter, the crossing point being a mile or two up the river.

It was even harder for me, as in the intervening centuries somebody had built a couple of sanatoria in the way. I parked furtively in the back yard of the nearer one before getting out for a look.

This was more like it. Inside the deep moat, Sigulda's ruins were still ruined. From a crumbling bastion I looked back at Turaida, whose new orange-red towers rising high above the river were, from a distance, admittedly spectacular.

In the centre of the walls, chairs were placed as in an auditorium; apparently concerts are held here. In the gatehouse, however, were altogether more ominous traces of human activity: a couple of workmen and a cement mixer. It looked as if Sigulda was set for the same treatment as Turaida. Would these builders, I wondered, use eggs and honey to bind their mortar, as did the mediaeval Knights?

All other exploration today was strictly to be carried out on wheels. I was fascinated by the concept of a winter sports centre in a low-lying river valley, and went to look for hard evidence.

It was for real. A road along the valley bottom, signed with little pin-men on skis, led to several ski-slopes. They were about two hundred yards long, running down the scarp to the river's edge. Most were quite shockingly eroded. The soil here seemed to be pure sand, with only the trees keeping it in place. On each strip cleared for ski-ing, enormous amounts of it had been washed down the hillside, to arrive in a huge dried pancake at the bottom. The slopes above, scarred with great crevasses and pits, looked remarkably similar to Latvian roads.

Half a mile more, and I came to a strange contraption. An enormous tube, high above the ground on metal pylons, ran a contorted path the length of the hillside between buildings at top and bottom. It took a moment for the truth to dawn. This wasn't some factory cooling device which had escaped planning permission... but the bobsleigh run. Actually, it was really rather splendid; it just spoiled the view a bit.

After such alpine mod cons, it was no surprise to find that Sigulda even has a cable car. It runs the width of the gorge above the bridge, linking the two villages. The stretch of water directly below is recommended for swimming. It was a recommendation I wasn't burning to take up. The Gauja runs deep brown here, rather like the colour of a Scots burn through peat hillside, but without the wholesome excuse.

All about the valley are hundreds of footpaths, clearly signed and well maintained, with wooden steps for the steep climbs. The area must be paradise for walkers, and, as so often before on this trip, I made a mental note to return in years to come. The visitors are well catered for with several large carparks. In one of these I spent the rest of the afternoon, planning routes for my return visit.

So far today, so good. A spot of optimism was in order.

*

The Gutmana Cave, one of many pitting the sides of the gorge, is the scene of a local legend. Moreover, the water from its spring is said to remove facial wrinkles. As mine had probably doubled over the last two months, this had to be worth a look.

People here tell the story of the beautiful Maija, the so-called Turaida Rose, who killed herself here rather than submit to a fate worse than death at the hands of an army officer. There are embellishments - a magic scarf, for instance - but the elements of the story are probably true. Maija was certainly a real figure, for she is buried near the castle church.

I found the cave across the road beside a neatly manicured park, with gaily painted pavilions for holiday-makers. A rustic bridge crossed the river under the pines, and led to the foot of the cliff. Here the cave mouth opened in a cleft some seven feet high, and scored with graffiti. Not just any old graffiti; covering every inch of space, these carvings were done by skilled hands, and included several coats of arms.

The stream issued from the back of the cleft, and fed a cistern before running off across the valley and losing itself in the Gauja. I put it to the test, but found the claims of its cosmetic value to be a shameless deception.

From there I idled up the valley in low gear, taking time to enjoy the glorious evening. Much of the Gauja Valley is National Park, from Sigulda as far as Valmiera, half-way to the Estonian border. All is Crusading Knight country; as well as Sigulda, there are castles at Valmiera and Cesis, the latter being the headquarters of the Livonian Order, an offshoot of the Knights of the Sword.

At Straupe the road passed a grand old manor house that wouldn't have been out of place in a English village. In fact, it wouldn't have been out of place anywhere, its eclectic jumble of architectural styles representing just about everywhere I had been so far: red brick, yellow brick, stone, red tile, a sweep of violin curves framing a creamy-yellow and white stuccoed face, squat bits, tall bits; and peeping out behind, a bell-tower that would have beautifully graced a Riga church. The low sun painted the whole picture afresh in the lily-pond, fringed with bulrushes, that lay serenely beneath the walls.

I made a circuit of both Cesis and Valmiera, looking for supper. There wasn't much left in the food box but tuna and baked beans.

Nowhere, though, could I find a restaurant. Valmiera at least managed a general store where I was able to get a few provisions, including tinned mushrooms for my vegetable withdrawal symptoms. Supper would be a bit brighter than yesterday's.

But later than planned: with hunger blunting my usual incisive route-finding faculties, I got lost twice leaving the town. The delay gave time for a re-think, and I decided to cut across to the Riga-Tallinn "motorway", instead of the minor crossing to Valga and Tartu I'd planned originally. Cutting off a dog-leg made a compromise on distance; more to the point, it would be ghastly to arrive at a small border post, only to be told it was for Latvian/Estonian nationals only.

I stopped a few miles along the road, after a very easy day and a short distance. It was high time to sort the van out - and track down the odours of decay. They came from the coolbox, whose contents had given up the ghost and turned to slop.

The Slovakian gas, however, had come up trumps, lasting much better than the English stuff; even if it was inclined to breathe fire and smoke a bit on a new bottle. And after reading my expensive newspaper I had floor covering again. It felt quite decadent to be wiping my feet on two dollars.

*

Again, the day began with the afternoon. No matter, though, as I had only to cross the border, however long it took, and get a few miles up the coast to Pärnu.

Just as well, for almost immediately I hit dirt track, which made progress slow and bumpy. The accumulating pile of international loose change on the dashboard made for a sort of rattle index, conveniently measuring the awfulness of the road.

An inviting river tempted me for a wash, the mosquitoes of the morning having been too bad to display an inch of bare flesh. Close to, the water looked a bit brown, but was still decidedly the loser by meeting me. A crowd of minnows gathered, calling all their friends for a look; they fled whenever I squeezed soap into the water, but quickly reassembled each time.

At the border, to my astonishment, there was only one car ahead of me. This being Latvia, however, we waited an hour, to play the game according to the rules. This time at least I was prepared, taking advantage of the delay to wash the van with water saved from the river. The front remained filthy; nothing short of a blowtorch would remove the thick layer of squashed mosquitoes stuck to it by their own, and of course other people's, blood.

By the time I got through, I would gladly have shed some of the guard's. The obligatory hour behind a barrier in front of a completely empty road was the last straw, and when it opened I'd become pretty well apoplectic. It was a good ten miles before I took in anything much about Estonia.

CHAPTER XVII: TOWERS OF ELSINORE

At times the summit of the high city flashed;

At times the spires and turrets half-way down

Pricked thro' the mist...

(Tennyson: Idylls of the King)

To enter Pärnu is to step back in time, into a middle class island holding its own among the remnants of an anti-bourgeois regime.

Its grid of wide, regular streets, with prosperous looking houses among avenues of lime and chestnut spikes, gave me an elusive sense of déjà-vu. At last I had it: I could have been back in Frinton. Families strolled unhurriedly towards the beach, feeding the analogy, and my imagination began to turn every woman pushing a pram into a nanny.

There are sanatoria here, too. Most are discreetly secluded in quiet parks; but right on the sea front was an elegant, colonnaded pile, whose ochre-coloured plastering hinted at its main function: mud baths.

I parked near some dunes, and followed the holidaymakers heading for the sea. This spot was coyly labelled "women's beach". How quaint, I thought, until I went further and saw why. Among the sandhills an assortment of naked females, most of whom were twenty years older than me and as many stone heavier, flaunted a collection of sagging boobs and buttocks that would have had Reubens covering his eyes. I clenched my teeth to keep my face straight and continued resolutely towards the sea, passing a reclining sunbather with so much sagging flesh that I had to look twice to see which way up she was lying.

The water looked surprisingly clear - eat your heart out, Frinton - and there were toddlers swimming. It must be safe to risk a paddle. No need to worry about my now-hairy legs, with this competition. Perhaps it wasn't the wisest place, though, to get the camera out.

The main beach, just a short drive away, was rather more decorous. Conservationists would have scowled at the permanent amusements fixed in the sand - climbing frames, badminton nets and a funfair among the dunes; but they gave out an innocent friendliness and welcome. A multitude of laughing children thought so, too.

*

Trust me to pick the hotel with road works starting at quarter to six in the morning. I woke up very sick, with serious doubts about the tap-water with which I'd been generously lubricating my sore throat all night; but it passed.

I staggered down to the van under the weight of a bag of wet washing and last night's supper things, trying not to drip or clank as I passed the reception desk. Breakfast was a bowl of porridge by the bank of the Pärnu River, right on the estuary. As it slid past on its way into the northern corner of the Gulf of Riga, the smell of the water upheld the Gulf's reputation for pollution. Blue and gleaming at a distance, it ran black and greasy close to. But the gulls and terns didn't seem to mind, and the reeds between the dunes were thick with warblers.

From Pärnu you can sometimes get a boat to Kihnu. This island, they say, is a piece of living history, where ancient runic verses are sung at festivals, and where many women still wear national dress. After much asking around, and at least three wild goose chases, I managed to find a boat that was actually going there.

It was a sort of tramp steamer, busy loading up with a motley assortment of goods and people. The captain was a rather disreputable, elderly man who looked a bit like a tramp himself.

Yes, he had room for me. When was he leaving? In about half an hour. Better and better. When was he coming back? He wasn't. And no, there was no other boat.

Much as I wanted to get to Kihnu, I had an appointment with the Tallinn ferry. It was one more thing that would have to wait for another year.

*

Pärnu's high street, Pühavaimo, was a glorious muddle of styles. Steep gables poked their elbows into the ribs of fat baroque curves above balconies, bow windows and a variety of overhangs. As in the outlying quarters of Vilnius, much was built in wood.

In search of money, I found four bored-looking girls in a deserted bank - first-floor, of course - who squinted in turn at my travellers' cheques as if they were in Chinese, before grudgingly cashing them at a punitive commission rate. "Cash" here meant the Estonian Kroon, abbreviated to EEK.

Feeling rich with my pocketful of eeks, I took a look around the shops on Pühavaimo. They were largely stocked with leather goods at amazingly low prices. Among the usual wallets, belts and cases were a few more unusual items. I was fascinated by thick notebooks in beautifully tooled, striated leather, bound with leather clasps, and bought several. The resulting hole in my money was scarcely noticeable.

The Tallinn road out of Pärnu broke all the rules hitherto, with clear signs. The roads were user-friendly in other ways, too; smart petrol stations taking credit cards, and restaurants with signs of life. Maybe here I'd get something to eat other than tuna and beans.

In fact the Estonian motorist was catered for in every way. Burning up the miles on the excellent, empty motorway I passed a girl whose back view showed skin-tight, glossy lycra black pants, sequined top and platinum-blonde hair. Glancing behind her at the van and expecting a male driver, she turned and stuck out her chest, to show a cross-over top framing bare breasts.

A westernised attitude, complete with its less wholesome attributes, is typical of Estonia. Even under Soviet rule, the country's proximity to Finland made it impossible to maintain a hygienic distance between its honest comrades and the decadent west. The ferry service was an umbilical cord between the Estonians and their Finnish cousins, and Finnish television gave a window on western development and world affairs.

The tendency of Estonians to look north and north-west is deeply rooted in history. While for centuries Lithuania and Latvia have been culturally influenced by Poland and Germany respectively, Estonia has had more than just racial links with Scandinavia over the last millennium.

A thousand years after the early Central Asian wanderers arrived here from their original homelands on the fringes of the Altai mountains, they were conquered for the first time by the Danes. After three centuries of Danish rule, during which several cities joined the Hanse, the Livonian Order of Knights bought out the Danes and rule passed to the south. But Estonia was to come under Scandinavian rule again, this time from Sweden. It wasn't until the early eighteenth century that Tsar Peter the Great broke Swedish power in the Great Northern Wars, and the Estonians fell under the Russian control from which they only emerged, briefly, between the two world wars... until 1991.

*

Today the Russian footing in Estonia, past and present, is viewed with a combination of resentment and tolerance.

In stilted English, often with a curious 1930's ring to it, the guide booklet "Tallinn This Week" deprecates the Soviet legacy with good humour and disarming frankness. "This guide is intended to protect you from the seamier side of life in our city that we have not been able to do away with, for we have been masters of our country for such a short time... there is an air of negligence which may depress you. Be sure to take a look at page 13."

So far, my impression of Tallinn was that it was the busiest Baltic capital; far from negligence, it had an air of direction and purpose. Traffic crammed the pulsating streets, and I had been lucky to find my way to a big hotel with an Intourist office. Clutching the little booklet that was my prize, I went back to sit in the van - and take a look at page 13.

"You're a lucky dog," I read, "if you manage to find a trolley in the air terminal. The porters hide them to make sure they get hired.... Another relic of Soviet times: the customer is always wrong." Shades of the bank clerklets in Pärnu.

"The Estonian telephone service is far and away not the best in the world. But keep your hair on, and think of the Tallinn citizen who has been waiting to have a phone installed since 1950!" Having now washed its hands of the bad bits, the booklet went on to bubble with information about Tallinn, from history to pop concerts via all the best places to see. "Happy landings!" it finished.

Thus braced, I plunged once more into the traffic and went looking for the ferry office to pick up my ticket.

Miraculously, the van found its way direct to the "Tallink" office on Roosenkrantsi street (no difficulty in remembering the address - just think of Guildenstern). But a notice on the door wiped off my satisfied smile. There was no service here. I should have gone direct to the quay.

No problem; as the focus of Tallinn's existence for a thousand years, the harbour was well signed. A pair of sloppy girls gave me my ticket and boarding pass, and I discovered only later that they had dated them wrongly. I could be sloppy, too; I just crossed out the date and wrote the right one over, and nobody ever questioned it.

Several times during these wanderings I caught sight of the old city; tantalising glimpses of walls, steeples and towers, seen briefly through the gaps between office blocks or factories. I firmly turned my back, for I absolutely had to recharge my legs a little before I could walk round it. The sunshine, meanwhile, was glorious. If the weather broke tomorrow I should curse myself.

Parkland surrounds the old quarter to the west. Finding a shady corner, I dipped into my guide book and planned for the next day. This was surely the most peaceful spot in Tallinn. The traffic was a distant hum, only the birds and the occasional shout of children breaking the silence. On the skyline reared the grey stone towers of the citadel above, mysterious, timeless, somehow benevolent.

*

The campsite was quiet, too. Once again I could pick my spot among the empty spaces, far from the few other customers.

I needed the peace, for I was really struggling. Almost hallucinating with exhaustion, I was seeing the world as if from the wrong end of a telescope. Since Sigulda I had suffered from mounting feverishness and night sweats, leaving me wringing wet for much of the night and horribly sticky by day. And now I was down to only six hours a day out of bed, consistently unable to start until early afternoon and then unwilling to spare more than an hour's rest to break the day.

At least my legs were still just about working. And the campsite had clean showers, a tap with a hose - and excellent food.

The tiny restaurant was a gem. Language was a problem, as I hadn't dared try my feeble Russian again after Turaida. But at least I could recognise solyanka and carbonnade from the menu, albeit with barely recognisable spelling. The first was soup with tomato, yogurt and spicy sausage. After the days of dwindling rations I thought I was in heaven, until the second course came and I knew I was. Instead of the expected stew came a melting, juicy cutlet, the best food my contracting stomach had seen throughout the trip.

It was a good omen. Moreover, I was at last back "on schedule". A good handful of aspirin and an early night, and I would surely be firing on all cylinders for the last couple of days.

*

In the days of the Hanse, Tallinn's skyline, with its galaxy of needle spires and turrets scattered over a hill by the sea, must have drawn incoming ships like a beacon.

Today, that view is obscured by a mass of high rise buildings, and insensitively placed industrial plants with which the Communists sought to modernise at any price. But the old quarter has survived largely unspoiled. Much of it would surely still be recognisable to the mediaeval merchants who once trod its winding, cobbled streets, and filled its warehouses with the best goods Europe could provide.

The greater part of its wall remains. It is a stark grey barrier, softened by glowing red tiles and broken, at intervals, by round towers with sharp conical roofs; Guy Fawkes rocket towers, seemingly held to earth only by the sheer

169

weight of their stones. The houses they enclose are those in which prosperous Hanseatic burghers once lived and stored their wares, some still bearing gantry and pulley under their narrow gables.

Surely this wasn't the twentieth century. It felt more like a setting for Hamlet. At any moment I expected to walk into the middle of a bloody duel, or look up to see the ghost of the old king drifting along the walls.

Children here ask, "Why is Tallinn lame? Because it has one Long Leg and one Short Leg!" The legs in question are respectively Pikk Jalg and Luhike Jalg, the two routes up to the castle hill, or Toompea. Pikk was the old route from the quay, via the Great Coastal Gate and its guardian tower, Paks Margareeta.

Fat Margaret is well named. Her sixteenth century walls are four metres thick, and intermittent attempts by cannonball on her virtue have produced no more impression than a slight freckling of her face over the centuries. Nowadays she houses the maritime museum. I visited mainly to climb to her roof and look out over the city, but once inside found myself captivated by the intricate models of old sailing ships which filled her three floors.

Close by is the Oleviste Church, whose spire, once one of the highest in Europe, was long used as a navigation marker by incoming ships. From its tip, they say, you can see Finland on a clear day.

From here I wandered among the old merchants' and guilds' houses on Pikk, halfway up to the castle; then, ducking into an alleyway past the Pühavaimu Church, emerged into the sunlight of the Raekoja Plats.

Straight ahead, across a hundred yards of cobblestone, stood the Old Town Hall for which the square is named. One of Tallinn's most famous landmarks, this is said to be Europe's only remaining Gothic town hall. The term "Gothic" suggested to me, in my ignorance, flights of fancy; but this hall was severely functional. The drabness of its grey stones, darkened with the dust of six centuries, was relieved only by a row of battlements above and arches beneath. And by the graceful curves of its tower, which looked as if it had been borrowed from another world. It came as no surprise to learn that this was a seventeenth century addition, and modelled on the architect's sketches of minarets after a visit to the Middle East. Strange contrast with the austerity below; Beauty and the Beast, I thought irreverently.

Just behind me was another landmark. The little shop was labelled "Raeapteek", or Council Apothecary; in Gothic lettering, of course. Still operating as a chemist's shop, it has done so continuously since at least 1422.

After a short detour to patronise the only public loo recommended by Tallinn This Week ("all others," it cautioned, "should be used only in case of dire need") I rejoined Pikk and began the long trudge up to Toompea.

It led me under a conical gatehouse and into the square of Lossi Plats, where the Russian Orthodox Cathedral, its onion domes looking hopelessly lost among the wealth of mediaeval straight lines, confronted the pink walls of the Castle. The latter, ever more palace than castle and now the seat of the fledgeling Estonian Parliament, was closed to the public. But, unlike the other locked churches I had passed today, the cathedral was open.

Seen as a symbol of Russian domination, the Alexander Nevsky Cathedral has never been popular. "It looks like a samovar," snorted a local writer, "and should be blown up." Estonians continue to regard Toomkirik, at the other side of the citadel and the oldest church in Tallinn, as the true cathedral.

Inside, the Russian church was typical of eastern Orthodox forms: cruciform but symmetrical, with no nave - just a huge central dome flanked by four smaller side ones. It reminded me of Hagia Sophia in Istanbul, and I half expected to see Arabic inscriptions; but instead there were icons, richly decorated with silver, and intricate hanging lanterns thick with dust.

Crossing the square to the rear of the Castle, I re-entered the Middle Ages. Across the lawns, the bastions of the oldest part stood out. The original work of the Danes had long vanished, but their successors, the Livonian Knights, built to last. Three of their towers remain, of which the tallest, Pikk (Tall) Hermann, was proudly flying the flag of the new Republic.

A hundred yards and a dramatic section of wall away down the hill was the biggest tower of them all. Kiek in de Kök means, in low German, "peep into the kitchen". It is so named because of its height; the watchmen looking over the city from its top were supposed to be able to peer down the chimneys into the hearths below.

It is open as a museum, with an assortment of old maps and some fascinating scale models of Tallinn at various times in history. The best exhibit, though, was the view. Even if the bit about the chimneys wasn't strictly true, the sight of the whole city laid out within the girdle of its mediaeval walls had to be the best throughout the Baltic Republics.

*

East of the Old Town, across Tallinn bay, is Pirita Beach, venue for the sailing events in the 1980 Olympics. It looks out to the north-west and Finland, and was spectacular this evening at sunset.

I took a drive through the parks and woods that here punctuate the more utilitarian bits of Tallinn. Just a few miles from the city centre was a beautifully quiet spot, where the Pirita river flowed rapid and shallow over rocks and under a bridge, before curving back under a sandy, pine-covered bank.

I sat a while under the bank by the river, and found I wasn't alone. It was a popular place for Tallinners to swim, fish, or just sit and think. Upstream was the perfect overnight spot, where a track met the road in a wide sweep of concrete that was almost a layby. It looked a highly suitable and entirely legal place to park.

Perhaps it wasn't legal after all. For later that night I had another Police visit. They drove up in a glare of headlights, and rattled the door-handle violently. I woke up quaking, and was almost relieved to see the flashing blue light. Before I could open up they were on their way, having decided that I was no threat to public order.

The locals weren't all hostile. For here again, and for the last time, the nightingales sang until I slept.

*

"You can't park here!" It was in Estonian, but perfectly clear.

His pal spoke English, and backed him up. I apologised, explaining my "when in Rome" principle; for the quiet side road leading towards the city walls was full of parked cars, and I could see nothing remotely resembling a "no parking" sign. So the two men - officials of some sort - explained a few local parking laws, many of which I'd been blithely breaking for weeks, and sent me to a spot not a hundred yards away where it was OK to leave the van.

By the time I walked back, all the cars up the lane were clamped. Ten minutes earlier, and the van would have been among them. For the rest of the day I used my new-found knowledge, and parked with extreme care.

Candy-striped awnings lined the hundred yards before the Viru Gate. Below were buckets of technicolour; the flower market was in progress. Around and behind, the trinket sellers had their barrows. At one of these, while bargaining for some amber, I heard the most unintelligible language yet. I listened covertly for fully half a minute before realising the speaker was Glaswegian.

He was the first of many. It turned out that Estonia was to play Scotland in the World Cup, and half Scotland had made the journey in support.

This, my last full day, was Christmas Shopping Day. But I also took time to explore some of the quieter corners of the Old Town. A surprise in its back streets was the abundance of trees. Huge trees crammed into impossibly tiny back yards, or bursting through cracks in the pavement; once, a bank of lilacs growing directly out of a first floor roof.

Here and there small, cramped shops overflowed with excellent leather goods, tourist kitsch, multi-coloured jewellery and more amber. In one alley I bought a Soviet Army cap for Mike from a man who led me furtively off the street and into a dark corner of a friendly shop. Black Market goods? I remembered how openly they sold such things in Berlin, and wondered if melodramatics were part of the sales pitch.

It would have been a pleasure to wander those lanes for days, buying something here, something there. But as usual my legs were walking to rule; so, trying not to despise my lack of imagination, I made for the State Department Store, for one large binge under a single roof. Estonia was always reputed to have the best range of consumer goods in the Soviet Union. How would things stand now?

Even this big department store worked on a counter-service only basis with masses of staff. My grandmother would have been at home here. Occasionally an abacus stood beside a primitive cash register, and only the shoe-department had wire baskets and a check-out.

The range of goods, though, was highly compatible with the nineties in all but price. Everything was a bargain and I bought presents for all, staggering out shamelessly some time later under several bags. With the last of my spare eeks I visited the music counter in search of something genuinely Estonian.

Two old ladies in national costume decorated the tape of folk music. It was a pity, I found later, that they were themselves the singers, squawking through both sides with voices like elderly daleks. But the Estonian part-songs were angelic; while an unusual recording of folk tunes played on a musical box was sheer good fun, and just the thing to listen to while bouncing the van over rough Tallinn streets at high speed.

*

Ask a foreigner what he remembers best about the struggle for independence in the Baltic, and he would probably reply: the Human Chain. The western media were delighted with the event, when some two million people joined hands to form a solid human wall stretching from Tallinn to Vilnius, a symbol of solidarity throughout the Baltic states against continuing Soviet rule.

Ask an Estonian the same question, though, and there is no doubt that he would answer: the Singing Revolution.

Song and folklore festivals have long been an integral part of Estonian culture, attracting enormous audiences. From 1987 onwards these became in effect Independence rallies, at which the crowds sang formerly banned songs and waved the old national flag.

There could be no more suitable vehicle for embryonic Estonian nationalism. For the choral heritage of Estonia matches that of Wales.

But it isn't only in choral music that Estonia excels. For such a small country it possesses more than its fair share of musical talent. The current generation alone has produced two giants: the internationally acclaimed conductor Neeme Järvi, and the composer Arvo Pärt, whose religious settings so irritated the Communist authorities. And Tallinn boasts a first-rate orchestra - less famous than it deserves, being rarely heard outside its native land.

So I was thrilled to find that the Estonian State Symphony Orchestra was to give a performance on my last night in Tallinn. At last my luck was in. I had missed by a few hours several tempting concerts along my way; here was compensation, and the perfect end to the trip.

The concert hall was almost new, attractively but unfussily furnished, with huge cut-glass chandeliers. The only jar in the decor was the appearance of the organ pipes, brassily uniform like shiny new plumbing. My ticket, for a front seat on the balcony, cost just fifteen eeks - about seventy-five pence.

It was the best fifteen bob's worth I've ever had. I'd never heard of the conductor or piano soloist, but between them they served up a delectable programme: a Chopin piano concerto followed by one of my favourites, the Andante Spianato and Grande Polonaise, in full orchestral setting. Half-time was followed by an electrifying performance of Tchaikovsky's Fourth Symphony, the brass making the hairs prickle on the back of my neck.

Leaving the hall afterwards, I was taken by surprise. Instead of darkness, the streets outside were still, at past ten, flooded with full light. I had forgotten the latitude; the sun was still soaring high above the horizon.

Just now, I knew exactly how it felt.

CHAPTER XVIII: HOME RUN

They change their sky, not their soul, who run across the sea.

(Horace: Epistolae)

The deck was shrouded in pea-soup fog. The contrast after weeks of clear Baltic sunshine was marked, and unmistakeable: this had to be western Europe again.

Travemünde lies at the very south-western tip of the Baltic, where the way west is barred by the peninsula joining Germany to Denmark. Nowadays a busy port in its own right, it grew up to serve the town of Lübeck, a few miles up the Trave River.

Centuries ago, the Trave hummed with shipping; for Lübeck was the first of the Hanseatic ports, and remained the nerve centre of the League throughout its history.

Straight after Riga and Tallinn, it should have felt like a home from home. But it was utterly foreign. There was none of the lightness and elegance of the Estonian spires, the intimacy of narrow streets framed by pastel coloured houses as in both capitals. Here, instead, was the parent of the solid, red-brick piles that sometimes oppressed Riga's charm. Lübeck was earthbound with its Prussian heaviness; fat, complacent and visibly worthy.

Not, in one respect, all that foreign. I was feeling pretty heavily earthbound, too.

*

I had hoped to see a little of Helsinki, if only from the road. To spend fourteen hours in Finland and do nothing there was inconceivable. But, in the event, that was exactly what happened. I had run my finish in Tallinn, and had absolutely nothing left.

The compulsory breathalyser on leaving the ferry had passed me safe to drive. But I found myself bumbling around mindlessly, without a clue where I was going. The last straw was to find white lines on the road again, after weeks of doing without. The effect on me, rather than clarity, was utter bewilderment; trying to find a way through them was worse than trying to find the correct relay changeover box in the psychedelic confusion of a well-marked running track. It took an extreme effort of will to pull myself together and replace the aimless rambling with some conscious decisions.

This was probably the lowest point of the whole trip. The drive and concentration, the energy and effort needed to keep me going had collapsed in a sort of vacuum of total exhaustion. It was obvious that there was no benefit in anything but to get fed and flat, in very short order.

I fetched up in a residential area, at the side of a highly respectable looking, middle class sort of street. What the residents thought of having a tramp parked on their doorsteps, I hardly cared to think. At least I kept the curtains tight shut to spare them the sight of the, by then, shambolic state of the van's interior.

*

Boarding the Travemünde ferry really felt like the beginning of the journey home. Besides the stirring of a bleary satisfaction, the main feeling was one of enormous relief at being able to switch off from any action or decision. I simply abandoned self and van to this huge floating juggernaut, which would do everything necessary for me, including think, for the next day and a half.

I spent twenty-eight of the next thirty hours in oblivion. Perhaps by the time I set foot on dry land, the long process of rebuilding and restoration might be under way.

*

But with the frenetic drive finally switched to "off", it was hard to move very far. I was grateful to find that it was permitted, this being Sunday, to drive under Lübeck's imposing gatehouse and park inside the walls.

Cobbled and paved streets led up to the centre. Here was the cathedral, of predictable red-brick topped by tall, heavy towers. Two curious spyholes peered over the town from the blank wall alongside. Behind the cathedral was the Town Hall, also red-brick but lightened by some elegant windows and a double row of arches at ground level.

I was glad of having walked this far, for just beyond I found Lübeck wearing an altogether friendlier face. In the angle between the two buildings lay the market square, where a Mediaeval Fair was just getting going.

Strips of bunting and flags of every colour defied the gloomy weather. Underneath, the market seethed with people, many in period dress. It wasn't hard to imagine the shades of the Hanse moving among the crowd under the buildings they had themselves raised, and looking on with satisfaction wherever a good bargain was struck.

*

The last drive was a short one, for it was only thirty miles up the road to Hamburg.

Out in the country, the verges were lush and the hawthorn in bloom. The farmland behind, here divided into fields, suddenly looked very English. I feared my subconscious would think itself already home, and had to chant a continuous mantra to remind myself to drive on the right.

Off the main road, a lane framed in wild lupins led me to a familiar woodland berth. During the night, the deer came out of the forest to wander round the van in a last farewell.

In the morning, Hamburg was five minutes away. And as I drove on to the homeward ship, there began the first stirrings of a surging euphoria.

AFTERTHOUGHT

Was it worthwhile? Would I do it all again? They were questions I asked myself all too often over the ensuing five months' inevitable relapse, while observing at length the capacity of The Beast to bear a grudge for a very long time.

It wasn't ever meant to be a holiday, I reminded myself. And if for more of it than I cared to remember, I had felt like Sisyphus eternally pushing his rock uphill - well, I shouldn't have kept overspending my resources.

But then, that was what it was all about. The substance of the journey, the signature of its reality, was not the daily plod but the transcendent moments: the Polish beavers, the canter with Equador, the ladders of the Sucha Bela. For a few glorious moments I had thumbed my nose at my enemy, and It had failed to hold me in thrall.

So yes, it was worth it.

And yes, emphatically yes, I would do it all again

APPENDIX: KNOW THINE ENEMY

"I live in a glass cage," wrote Dr. Clare Fleming* of her experience as an ME sufferer. " Often I seem to be well, so only those close to me see the extent of my disability. Indeed, within my prison of inactivity, there are moments when I feel relatively well. Yet the invisible walls around me are impenetrable. Beyond them lies a barrage of symptoms, and the further I push myself, the greater the deterioration, and the longer the recovery time: hours, days, even weeks....I long to surge ahead, but my glass cage, though expanding, remains firmly in place, and any attempt to break through it is penalised with a setback. I started like Aesop's hare and have had to learn to be a tortoise."

ME, (or Myalgic Encephalomyelitis**, to give it its party name, for the only time in these pages), is seen as an illness of the late twentieth century. Yet it is undoubtedly no newcomer to the human picture, even if it has barely as yet made the pages of the medical textbooks.

The capacity to categorise and minutely define illness is a feature of recent times; in past centuries it was often a mystery what caused an individual to "go into a decline" or "become an invalid". But among some of the more famous invalids, some details of whose ailments were recorded along with their lives, there is here and there documentary evidence giving a strong indication of ME. Just as we can nowadays say with reasonable certainty that Julius Caesar was epileptic and Henry VIII died of syphilis, it is also highly probable that, to give a couple of examples, Charles Darwin and Florence Nightingale were both victims of ME

The sharp rise in incidence of ME in recent years is, like the rise in childhood asthma, the phenomenon of "sheep-dip 'flu" or Organo-Phosphate poisoning, and the drop in male fertility, possibly linked to environmental causes. Until a great deal more research has been done, however, it is impossible to be sure.

For until recently, knowledge of ME was limited by a Catch-22 situation of monumental absurdity. When little was known about it, a baffled medical establishment could continue to deny its very existence as a specific illness. And of course, if it didn't exist, there was no point in spending money to study it.

It wasn't until the two groups, the ME Association and Action for ME, had

*please see Acknowledgements
**known in the USA as CFIDS, or Chronic Fatigue & Immune Dysfunction Syndrome

built up sufficient funds to finance research that any investigation into ME could begin in this country; to this day there is no government funding for laboratory research. And so it has taken years to shed the tabloid "Yuppie 'Flu" image, the abiding impression of many people and not a few doctors, that there is no more to it than a sort of glorified tiredness.

So what is it really, this elusive plague that has been estimated to affect up to a quarter million people in the U.K. alone?

ME is now believed to be a neurological illness, its immediate cause usually being abnormal response to a viral infection, which may be something as simple as a cold or 'flu. It shows itself in a bewildering variety of symptoms, which for the luckiest may fade within a year or two, while the more unfortunate - that is, the majority - endure them for life.

First and foremost is debility. Strength and stamina are impaired, and what remains vanishes with indecent haste on activity, taking disproportionately long to replenish. Capacity may vary from the ability, say, to walk a mile down to the inability to feed yourself or walk to the loo. Approximately 20% of those with ME are bedridden for many years.

Secondly, a corresponding blocking of mental faculties: of co-ordination, concentration, memory and so on. Blurred vision may prevent you from reading, or even watching TV; while slurred speech and an inability to walk in straight lines may be misconstrued by those who don't know you're ill.

Thirdly, there is often a great deal of pain. While most experience aches and pains similar to those of 'flu, many sufferers have constant, sometimes severe pain in muscles and joints.

These are the definitive signs. But further biochemical and neurological oddities confuse the issue, with a thousand and one permutations of diverse and often bizarre symptoms: frightening heart problems, acute skin sensitivity, hallucinatory dreams, the embarrassment of hot flushes... the list could go on and on. Food allergies may become a problem, while alcohol intolerance, cruelly, is almost universal.

Emerging theories shed spots of light here and there. Current research indicates viral damage to muscle and brain cells, notably the hypothalamus; while brain scans show consistently reduced blood supply to specific parts of the brain, including, again, hypothalamus. Lack of oxygen here accounts very plausibly for some of ME's stranger symptoms. Although ME is currently internationally classified as a neurological illness, the jury is still out as to whether its neurological symptoms are primary or secondary. An increasing number of experts argue convincingly for a viral agent, probably a mutation of the polio enterovirus.

There is no standard medical treatment at all, except occasionally that which will alleviate individual symptoms. Many people turn to holistic medicine, finding that, for example, homeopathy or acupuncture may improve overall health status, enabling the body to fire strengthened resources at the invader. Others modify their diet, obtaining relief by avoiding food causing intolerance or allergy.

Relaxation techniques, meditation or hypnotherapy are also used to counter the psychological effects of long-term illness. For with such a destructive enemy these are legion: intense frustration, fear of the future, constant sense of failure and loss of all feeling of self-worth being only a few. Worst of all, perhaps, a disorientating loss of the sense of your very identity, since who and what you are is almost totally defined by what you do - or did, and can do no longer.

And so we come to what was, for many years, one of the most frightening aspects of ME. For in the days of ignorance, these last signs threw a lifeline to many doctors, baffled by an illness for which there is no diagnostic test, no irrefutable proof in test tube or on screen, not even a helpful rash of purple spots. "Clinical depression" was entered on many a medical record; psychosomatic disorders, repressed childhood fear, even agoraphobia being pinned on the unfortunate victim. Frustration, fear, failure, loss of self-worth? You're the victim of psycho-social dislocation, you were told, in a glib confusion of cause and effect. Now we've got you pigeon-holed, don't worry: once your mind is straightened out, of course your body will function normally again. Here's your letter of referral; the shrink is the second door on the left.

"To have ME," wrote novelist and former yachtswoman Clare Francis in 1989, "is to experience hell twice over, firstly through the devastation of the disease itself, and secondly through the lack of diagnosis, information and support that most sufferers are still having to endure... family and friends found it difficult to understand a disease which had no name, no visible symptoms, makes you come apart mentally, yet often leaves you looking perfectly well. Rather than test their loyalty beyond reasonable bounds, I pretended my illness wasn't happening. I covered up the gaping holes in my life with lies and evasions: while I slept all day my answering machine said I was out; when I stumbled over words or walked into things I joked about having had a late night; and my social life was reduced to almost nothing by constantly pleading a previous engagement. I began to live the life of a recluse - a lonely, isolated and desperate recluse."

It was the weakest and the inarticulate who really suffered; at best unable to work but often deprived of social security benefits, at worst subjected, with much good intention but little sensitivity, to such "cures" as enforced physiotherapy. And things could be even worse for children. Twelve-year-old Ean Proctor, paralysed and mute from his illness, was forcibly taken away by social workers from his parents, who were accused of being over-protective in contesting a psychiatric diagnosis. Therapists dropped Ean in the deep end of a swimming pool, genuinely believing that they could shock him into regaining the use of his arms and legs. When they fished him out as he was going down for the third time, they were finally convinced.

Nowadays, thank heaven, the medical world wears a kinder face. The World Health Organisation listed ME as a neurological illness in 1992, after which time it began to be "recognised" in Britain. Nowadays most doctors are helpful and informative, although a few remain who have nailed their colours too firmly - and too publicly - to the psychiatric mast to haul them down again.

And at last the label of ME ceased to be a stigma, and became respectable.